Praising
the God
of Grace

Praising the God of Grace

The Theology of Charles Wesley's Hymns

Participant

CHARLES YRIGOYEN JR.

Abingdon Press
Nashville

PRAISING THE GOD OF GRACE
THE THEOLOGY OF CHARLES WESLEY'S HYMNS

This book is printed on acid-free paper.

Library of Congress Cataloging-in-Publication Data

Yrigoyen, Charles, 1937–
    Praising the God of grace : the theology of Charles Wesley's hymns
    p. cm.
    Includes bibliographical references.
    ISBN-0-687-03810-3
    1. Wesley, Charles, 1707-1788. 2. United Methodist Church
    (U.S.)—Hymns—History and criticism. 3. Hymns, English—History and criticism. I. Title.

BV415.A1Y75 2005
264'.23'092—dc22

2004024180

ISBN 13: 978-0-687-03810-7

08 09 10 11 12 13 14—10 9 8 7 6 5 4 3

MANUFACTURED IN THE UNITED STATES OF AMERICA

For

Members of the General Commission on Archives and History
The United Methodist Church
Past and Present

Who blessed me with the opportunity to serve the church I love

Contents

Preface

I have been a Methodist and then a United Methodist all my life. My love and respect for Methodism's history, message, and ministry began with my parents' teaching. Furthermore, throughout childhood and adolescence and then as a pastor, college chaplain, teacher, and denominational agency executive, I have been acquainted with countless Methodists and United Methodists who have confirmed for me the beauty and significance of the Wesleyan/Methodist tradition.

Sunday school classes, summer camps, youth groups, worship services, annual conferences, and a variety of church meetings are "Methodist" places where I have been accepted, challenged, encouraged, and nurtured. I am humbly, but unashamedly, Wesleyan "to the bone."

Over the years my appreciation for the hymns of Charles Wesley has deepened as a result. I have found myself pondering more thoroughly the message about, and praise of, the Triune God through Wesley's poetry. His life and hymns have immensely enriched my understanding of the Christian faith, especially my worship.

With gratitude for Wesley's life and ministry, I am pleased to share something of his work with the readers of this book. The debt I owe to friends and colleagues for this opportunity is enormous. A few of them are especially important. The General Commission on Archives and History of The United Methodist Church, for whom I work, provided the study leave to make possible most of the research that forms the basis for the book. Iain D. Murton at Wesley House,

Cambridge, England, and Peter Forsaith, the Wesley Centre, Oxford Brookes University, Oxford, England, arranged hospitality and comfortable quarters during the study leave. My friends Kenneth E. Rowe and John R. Tyson read parts of the manuscript and provided helpful comments. Any and all flaws, of course, remain my responsibility. It is my hope that this book will enable you, the reader, to begin to recognize the amazing ministry of Charles Wesley and to pay closer attention to the content of his hymns.

Introduction

Millions of Christians regularly sing his hymns without knowing much about him. "Hark! the Herald Angels Sing," "Christ, the Lord, Is Risen Today," and "O For a Thousand Tongues to Sing" are among the most popular. These and his many other hymns are sung by individuals and congregations of every major Christian denomination. His hymns are one of the greatest treasures Methodism shares with the world. We are speaking, of course, about Charles Wesley (1707–1788). This book celebrates the life, ministry, and hymnody of this hymn writer. With his brother John, Charles Wesley was one of the foremost leaders of the revival in eighteenth-century England in which the Methodist movement was born and in which the ministry and worship of Christianity was changed forever.

Purposes of Charles Wesley's Hymns

Charles Wesley's hymns express his personal experience and spirituality. Although many of them undoubtedly provided an aid for his private meditation, prayer, and praise, perhaps to be used only by himself, the vast body of his hymns, numbering in the thousands, was intended to be sung by groups of Christians gathered for worship and fellowship. Wesley's hymns have at least three purposes.

(1) They provide a wealth of texts for individuals and congregations to offer songs of praise, confession, thanksgiving, and petition

to the Triune God. Nothing exceeds the importance of worship. It is the primary way we recognize God's presence among us, render our gratitude for his love, and seek his guidance for our lives. Charles Wesley's hymns are intended to assist us in worshiping God as we should.

(2) Wesley's hymns, thoroughly grounded in the Bible and Christian doctrine, are an instrument for teaching Scripture and setting forth and explaining basic Christian belief. Virtually every line of every hymn is related to a passage in the Bible. Biblical stories and verses are the foundation of his poetry. Since Scripture is central to the hymns, it is not surprising that they also set forth the central beliefs of the Christian faith. Wesley's hymns are a primer on the Bible and Christian beliefs. They help us sing the biblical story and our faith.

(3) Wesley's hymns clearly delineate an evangelical approach to Christianity that centers on God's grace, especially revealed in the life, atoning death, resurrection, and ascension of Jesus. Grace exposes the ways we fail God and one another, frees us to repent and receive God's pardon, and leads us to holiness of heart and life, that is, loving God with all we are and have and loving our neighbors as ourselves.

Where to Find Charles Wesley

A number of sources help us comprehend Charles Wesley's knowledge and practice of the Christian faith effectively clarified in his hymns. Among them are the following:

(1) The extant sections of his journal that describe much of his life from March 9, 1736, to November 5, 1756. Although it is unfortunate that we do not have more of Wesley's personal journal, the sections we possess deal with the critical period of his mission to Georgia, return to England, conversion experience, and the earlier years of his leadership in the Methodist movement. The reprint of his journal may be viewed on the Web site listed in the bibliography at the end of this book (pp. 109-10).

(2) A large collection of letters that Wesley wrote to others. These letters reveal much about his personal life as a student, husband, and father, as well as his role in the formation and development of the Methodist movement. A helpful introduction to the letters is Frank Baker's book on Wesley's letters, listed in the bibliography.

(3) A small selection of the thousands of sermons he preached. Charles Wesley was apparently an outstanding preacher whose messages changed the lives of many. His preaching was biblical, clear, and uncomplicated. The few surviving sermons have been collected in one volume, edited by Kenneth G. C. Newport, listed in the bibliography.

(4) Wesley's hymns and poems. The number of Wesley's hymns and poems is staggering. Estimates range from six thousand to nine thousand. Wesley wrote the words, not the music, for his hymns. Contrary to a widely circulated belief, his hymn-poems were not set to popular tavern tunes of his time. Regrettably, fewer and fewer of his hymns are found in modern Methodist hymnals and songbooks. Many collections of his work exist, however, some edited by his brother John. Facsimile reprints of a few of his hymnbooks have been produced by the Charles Wesley Society and may be purchased from them. The locations in hymnbooks in which the hymn texts may be found are noted after the text of each hymn cited in this book, except for the theme hymns. These hymnbooks are also mentioned in the bibliography. Although Wesley's language and spelling has been retained in most of the hymns cited, in some cases it has been modernized. If it has been modernized, the text is noted as altered.

(5) Other sources, including letters to Wesley and comments about him in his brother John's writings and references to him by various other writers and commentators.

Although there are a few readable biographies of Charles, the definitive biography is yet to appear.

What Follows

The eight chapters of this book focus on eight of Charles Wesley's hymns that illustrate main themes of the Christian faith, including grace, the Triune God, the Christian life, the church, the Lord's Supper, and Christian hope. Each chapter begins with the words of a Wesley hymn, the theme hymn, the music for which is found on the compact disk included in the *Leader's Guide*. The main texts of the chapters are an invitation to think about the content of the theme hymns. Relevant Scripture passages from the New Revised Standard Version of the Bible and other Wesley hymn texts are included in each chapter to explain the meaning and Wesleyan context of the theme hymn. The Appendix contains a brief account of Charles Wesley's life. Reading this material first will give the reader a useful context in which to place him, his ministry, and his hymns. Its placement at the end of the book allows readers who want to study the hymns only to do so. Suggested questions for reflection and study are found at the end of each chapter in addition to those found in the separate *Leader's Guide*. The books listed in the bibliography also provide opportunities for further study for those who want to learn more about the richness of Wesley's hymns and poetry.

Chapter 1

Praising the God of Grace

1. *O for a thousand tongues to sing*
   my great Redeemer's praise,
   the glories of my God and King,
   the triumphs of his grace!

2. *My gracious Master and my God,*
   assist me to proclaim,
   to spread through all the earth abroad
   the honors of thy name.

3. *Jesus! the name that charms our fears,*
   that bids our sorrows cease;
   'tis music in the sinner's ears,
   'tis life, and health, and peace.

4. *He breaks the power of canceled sin,*
   he sets the prisoner free;
   his blood can make the foulest clean;
   his blood availed for me.

5. *He speaks, and listening to his voice,*
   new life the dead receive;
   the mournful, broken hearts rejoice,
   the humble poor believe.

6. *Hear him, ye deaf; his praise, ye dumb,*
   your loosened tongues employ;
   ye blind, behold your Savior come,
   and leap, ye lame, for joy.

7. In Christ, your head, you then shall know,
shall feel your sins forgiven;
anticipate your heaven below,
and own that love is heaven.

This hymn, written in 1739, is one of Charles Wesley's best known and most loved. He titled it "For the Anniversary Day of One's Conversion" to commemorate his "personal Pentecost," his conversion on May 21, 1738. The hymn may have been inspired by a conversation Wesley reportedly had with his influential Moravian friend, Peter Böhler. Speaking of God whose love is revealed in Jesus Christ, Böhler reportedly said, "Had I a thousand tongues, I would praise him with them all!"

Since its appearance in the popular and widely circulated hymn-book *A Collection of Hymns for the Use of the People Called Methodists*, published in 1780, "O For a Thousand Tongues to Sing" has appeared as the first hymn in many Methodist hymnals. Originally, the hymn had eighteen stanzas. A lot of vocal energy would be required of any congregation determined to sing them all. Many of today's hymnbooks do not include all the stanzas, although their substance is important. The stanza with which we are most familiar, the first stanza above, is the seventh stanza of the original.

The Wondrous Mystery of God's Grace

Every stanza of "O For a Thousand Tongues to Sing," a hymn of praise, joyously extols the forgiveness and new life God offers us in the redemptive sacrifice of Jesus on the cross. In order to appreciate the depths of such joy, it is necessary to understand the troublesome and serious state in which we live.

Following the teaching of Scripture, Charles Wesley identified the basic problem of human nature as sin, a topic that we often prefer to disregard because we are reluctant to think of ourselves as sinners. The biblical writers described sin as "missing the mark," failing to be the people God intends us to be, and, therefore, missing life's fullest blessings. We have only to look deeply within and around us to find the evidence of how we "miss the mark." The list of our personal and social offenses against others and God is staggering: Betrayal of trust. Vengeance. Exploitation of others for personal gain. Readiness for violence and war. Failure to act on behalf of the poor and helpless. Reluctance to pray and attend worship. We each can add to this list countless personal instances of doing what is wrong and failing to do what is right. The inventory of the ways we wound others and fail to attend to their needs is almost inexhaustible. When we survey the human community in which we live and probe deeply into our personal motives, words, and acts, we are sharply reminded that we "miss the mark."

Charles Wesley identified the problem of sin in himself and observed it in others. In his sermon on Romans 3:23-25, he pronounced sin a reality that has afflicted the human race since its beginning. No one is exempt from this universal problem (Romans 3:23).

According to Wesley, sin may be described in two ways. First, it is breaking the law of God. All of us stand before God as lawbreakers who do what God forbids and who fail to do what God requires. We not only do what is wrong; we also resist doing what is right. As lawbreakers, we stand in great peril not only in our relationships with others, but also in our relationship with God whose law we defy. As a result, our lives are impoverished and we incur God's judgment and wrath.

The penalty we deserve for breaking the law is not God's intention for us, however. God is always ready to pardon those who turn to him in repentance and faith. For that reason, Wesley penned an exhortation to those standing in jeopardy of God's judgment and, therefore, in need of God's forgiveness and reconciliation. The hymn is about repentance. The text reminds us that repentance entails more than merely being sorry for our lawbreaking. It calls for reorienting (turning) our lives to accept God's pardon and living in a way that pleases God and brings us new life:

Sinners, turn, why will you die?
God, your Maker, asks you why.
God, who did your being give,
Made you with himself to live;
He the fatal cause demands,
Asks the work of his own hands,
Why, ye thankless creatures, why
Will you cross his love, and die?
(A Collection of Hymns, #6)

3

Sin is not simply lawbreaking. Wesley also described it as a grave spiritual disease that infects us. Sin overspreads our lives, seeking to choke out what is good and right. Like an acute illness, it holds us in an oppressive grip that prevents us from enjoying life at its best in God's presence and favor. Another Wesley hymn, this one a prayer, seeks healing from the malady of sin:

> *Speak, gracious Lord, my sickness cure,*
> *Make my infected nature pure;*
> *Peace, righteousness, and joy impart,*
> *And pour thyself into my heart.*
> (A Collection of Hymns, #127)

Whether as lawbreaking or a spiritual disease, sin is the most serious reality with which human beings must come to terms. It creates disorder in us and in the human community. Sin threatens our relationships with others and with God and prevents us from enjoying God's abundant gifts. Who can reconcile us, heal us of our infirmity, and prepare us for life's fullest enrichment? The answer is clear. The God of grace provides all that is necessary. Our theme hymn praises the gracious God. In some ways it is a commentary on divine grace, God's unearned, unmerited, undeserved love. Although for Wesley, salvation was the work of all three persons of the Triune God, major emphasis in this hymn is placed on Jesus' sacrificial death from which flows forgiveness, new life, joy, and peace. The hymn speaks about Jesus as "my gracious Master" and mentions "the triumphs of his grace."

Although the grace that Wesley described is most prominently displayed in Jesus' death, it is also the distinguishing feature of the broader biblical story of God's relationship with his people. From the Bible we learn that creation was an act of the God of grace. The Exodus of the Hebrew people from their Egyptian slavery was God's gracious act. The covenant God established with the Hebrews and the constancy with which God maintained the covenantal relationship in faithful provision and patient forgiveness are evidence of divine grace and loving-kindness (Isaiah 54:10; Jeremiah 9:24). The biblical story proceeds with Jesus speaking about, and acting on behalf of, a gracious, caring God. His death by crucifixion not only disclosed the depth of God's love for us, but also is the means by which reconciliation with God and the restoration of spiritual health take place. The earliest Christians, especially the apostle Paul, persisted in celebrating the presence and work of God's love. Grace remains the bedrock of our relationship with God and all creation, so much of which is a gift. Furthermore, God's grace, so well described in the Bible, is also the dominant theme of the Methodist movement pioneered by John and Charles Wesley. At one place, Charles stated, "What'er we are, we are by grace." It is not surprising that his hymns pay tribute to God's extraordinary grace.

Stanza two of our theme hymn addresses Jesus as "My gracious Master and my God." In this hymn and many others, Wesley affirmed that Jesus is the enfleshment of the God of grace. With the biblical writers, Wesley announced that God has come among us in Jesus. God's "Word became flesh and lived among us, and we have seen his glory, the glory as of a father's only son, *full of grace* and truth" (John 1:14, emphasis added). If we want to know the nature of God's grace, what it is and how it works, we are urged to study Jesus' life and ministry and to pay special attention to his sacrificial, atoning death on the cross and his resurrection from the dead.

The grace, or love, of God is something wondrous, freely given. That is the nature of grace. This truth is often difficult for us to understand since we live in a world that is not accustomed to receiving what is valuable freely. We are more acquainted with earning or deserving what we have. We earn our grades at school. Promotions at work are granted on the basis of our productivity. Retirement benefits are calculated on what we have earned and saved over the years. God's grace, without which we cannot fully live, is not like that. It is wondrously and amazingly offered without our meriting or earning it. Grace offers abundant life without exacting a price (Isaiah 55:1). God's amazing grace is extolled in our theme hymn.

God's wondrous grace is also a mystery. Why does God love us? There is a great disparity between what God wants us to be and the many ways we "miss the mark" by how we think and act. Why is God so patient with us? Why is God always ready to forgive? What prompts God to offer us new life? Neither Wesley, nor we, can account for, or explain, the marvelous presence of God's steadfast love. No matter how deeply we offend or reject God, divine love is always ready to absorb and pardon the pain our sins inflict. It is always prepared to reconcile and restore us to God's favor. That is the mystery of the grace Wesley accepted and in which our theme hymn rejoices. Many of his hymns confess the mystery of God's grace, especially the grace apparent in Jesus' reconciling, atoning death. In one hymn, Wesley stated that even angels are astounded by this demonstration of the mystery of divine grace:

> *'Tis myst'ry all: th'Immortal dies!*
> *Who can explore his strange design?*
> *In vain the first-born seraph tries*
> *To sound the depths of love divine.*
> *'Tis mercy all! Let earth adore!*
> *Let angel minds inquire no more.*
> *(A Collection of Hymns, #193)*

Although the hymn "O For a Thousand Tongues to Sing" speaks primarily about the wondrous and mysterious grace of God in the forgiveness and reconciliation offered to us in Jesus Christ, Wesley knew that we encounter divine grace daily in countless ways, some obvious, others less noticeable. When someone is gracious to us, treats us better than we deserve, it is a sign of God's grace-full presence among us. The strength to survive difficult situations, the wisdom to choose what is right, the determination to seek reconciliation with someone from whom we are estranged—these are evidence of God's grace at work in our lives. In extraordinarily important moments, as well as in life's routine events, the mysterious presence of God's grace is freely furnished in immeasurable and often unrecognized ways.

How are we to respond to God's grace? We accept it with thanksgiving and offer songs of praise to the God of pardoning and renewing grace. In our thoughts, words, and acts we are moved to spread the good news of divine grace "through all the earth abroad." Furthermore, as God's grace treats us better than we deserve, we are prompted to be gracious to others (Matthew 18:23-35). When we consider the wondrous mystery of God's grace, we remember Peter Böhler's statement, "Had I a thousand tongues, I would praise him [God] with them all!"

The Nature and Work of God's Grace

Our theme hymn not only rejoices in the wondrous mystery of God's grace, but also describes what grace accomplishes with special emphasis on the reconciling nature of Jesus' death. Against the backdrop of the desperately sinful human situation, Wesley discloses what divine grace accomplishes.

(1) Grace forcefully subdues the fear of God's judgment and quiets the profound despair of those who realize their dangerously sinful condition (stanza three). Those who recognize the seriousness of "missing the mark" rightly fear the consequences. They stand under God's judgment and impending punishment. For those who turn to God in repentance, who trust in the atoning work of Christ, and who pledge by God's grace to live a new life, however, God's judgment is set aside; and there is no reason for despair.

When Wesley wrote that Jesus' name "charms our fears, [and] bids our sorrows cease" (stanza three), he was speaking not idly about the Savior's name, but about the power of the One who bears the name. In the ancient world, a person's name not only distinguished one individual from another. The name also represented the nature and power of the person who bore it. Jesus' name literally means "God saves" (Matthew 1:21). Jesus is the embodiment of saving grace. For who he is and the gracious redemption he achieves for us make his name "music in the sinner's ears." We sing about Jesus, the one who has come among us as the bearer of "life, and health, and peace."

(2) Grace possesses the power to overcome the disastrous power and effects of sin (stanza four). Sin holds us in a grip that makes us its slaves and keeps us from being the persons God intends us to be, people who are created to enjoy his presence and blessings by living in community with him and with one another. Sin hardens our hearts against God and our neighbors. The image of hard "hearts of stone" appears often in Wesley's hymns. In a hymn that emphasizes repentance, Wesley wrote:

> *Jesus, on me bestow*
> *The penitent desire;*
> *With true sincerity of woe*
> *My aching breast inspire;*
> *With softening pity look,*
> *And melt my hardness down;*
> *Strike, with thy love's resistless stroke,*
> *And break this heart of stone!*
> (A Collection of Hymns, #99)

Sin insists that we think, say, and do what and when we want regardless of the consequences for our relationships with God and others. Motivated by pride and self-will, sin will not yield to God's love and resists authentic love for God and others. Sin makes us satisfied to be quarrelsome, envious, vengeful, uncaring about others' circumstances, and unwilling to worship and serve God. Who can deliver us from our bondage to sin? The answer is clear. The God of grace working through the redemptive work of Jesus breaks the power of sin and "sets the prisoner free," that is, sets *us* free to respond to God's call to a better life.

Jesus is called "my great Redeemer" in the first stanza. Referring to him as "Redeemer" had a special meaning in the ancient world. Redemption often referred to the process of purchasing the freedom of a slave. The one who paid the purchase price was called the *redeemer,* a term frequently used in the Bible to describe God's role in delivering the people from captivity and bondage to sin (Isaiah 49:7; Jeremiah 50:34). Jesus, the enfleshment of God, is the Redeemer who purchased our freedom by his death on the cross and his victorious resurrection. The imagery of redemption and emancipation from slavery to sin is prominent in a stanza of another of Wesley's hymns:

> *Long my imprisoned spirit lay,*
> *Fast bound in sin and nature's night.*
> *Thine eye diffused a quick'ning ray;*
> *I woke; the dungeon flamed with light.*
> *My chains fell off, my heart was free,*
> *I rose, went forth, and followed thee.*
> *(A Collection of Hymns, #193)*

Wesley also thought of sin as stain and impurity. Sin leaves a mark on us that defaces life and mars the image of God in us. Who can cleanse the blight of sin and renew God's image in us? Wesley answered that God's grace in the sacrificial death of Jesus "can make the foulest clean."

(3) Grace brings new life (stanza five). When Wesley declared that Jesus "speaks, and listening to his voice, new life the dead receive," he was thinking more about those who are dead in their sin than those who are physically dead. This stanza echoes Wesley's sermon, "Awake, Thou That Sleepest" (1742), in which he spoke about those who are "dead unto God, 'dead in trespasses and sins.'" They are "dead to God and all the things of God; having no more power

to perform the actions of a living Christian than a dead body to perform the functions of a living man." God's grace in Christ offers these people new life. It breathes new life into them. They have personal experience of God's presence and are "a new creation" (Galatians 6:15). Under the guidance of God's Holy Spirit, they live a different life, a life of holiness. Those broken by the realization of sin's peril and destruction and who mourn their condition rejoice in God's pardoning grace. Persons who humbly recognize the poverty of their spiritual condition apart from divine grace find new life as they trustfully accept God's pardoning love.

(4) God's grace is universal (stanza six). It is available to all no matter who they are or what their circumstances. That is the theme of stanza six, which is based on two scriptural passages. The first is from the Old Testament. Speaking of God's promise of a future age, the writer said, "Then the eyes of the blind shall be opened, / and the ears of the deaf unstopped; / then the lame shall leap like a deer, / and the tongue of the speechless sing for joy" (Isaiah 35:5-6). The second passage contains Jesus' announcement that the future age reported in Isaiah had arrived in Jesus' ministry. Jesus said, "Go and tell John [the Baptist] what you hear and see: the blind receive their sight, the lame walk, the lepers are cleansed, the deaf hear, the dead are raised, and the poor have good news brought to them" (Matthew 11:4-5). God's grace is for all. It reaches out for the talented, prosperous, and renowned, as well as for the forgotten, ignored, and desperate. Everyone needs divine grace, and to everyone such grace is offered. This good news is stated in numerous Wesley hymns, including the following hymn of invitation:

> *Come, sinners, to the gospel feast;*
> *Let every soul be Jesu's guest;*
> *Ye need not one be left behind,*
> *For God hath bidden all mankind.*
>
> *Sent by my Lord, on you I call;*
> *The invitation is to all:*
> *Come, all the world; come, sinner, thou!*
> *All things in Christ are ready now.*
>
> *Come, all ye souls by sin oppressed,*
> *Ye restless wanderers after rest;*
> *Ye poor, and maimed, and halt, and blind,*
> *In Christ a hearty welcome find.*

. . . .

My message as from God receive:
Ye all may come to Christ, and live.
O let his love your hearts constrain,
Nor suffer him to die in vain!

. . . .

This is the time: no more delay!
This is the acceptable day;
Come in, this moment, at his call,
And live for him who died for all!
(A Collection of Hymns, #2, *emphasis added*)

We may not think it was unusual for Wesley to emphasize that God's saving grace is offered to everyone. Yet a school of thought in his time associated with the theology of John Calvin, a sixteenth-century Protestant reformer, held that God's pardoning grace is not offered to everyone. Calvin and his followers believed that sin totally destroyed human free will. They held that sin's corruption makes it impossible to respond freely to God's offer of forgiveness and salvation. Therefore, God decreed even before their birth who would be granted pardon and new life and who would not. Both John and Charles Wesley vehemently opposed this position, sometimes called "predestination," a position they believed was based on a misreading of Romans 8:28-30.

The Wesleys believed that the plain message of the Bible is that all people, by God's grace, are free to accept or reject God's offer of salvation. Such freedom is made possible by God's "preventing grace," God's grace free for all and free in all. What Wesley called "preventing grace," we refer to as "prevenient grace," literally, the grace that goes before. This grace, Charles Wesley affirmed, makes salvation possible for all. Sections of his journal and many of his hymns make clear that the denial of human free will is contrary to Scripture. At one place he called the repudiation of such freedom "satanic sophistry." Rather, he claimed, God's pardoning grace is universal, available to all.

Assurance and Anticipation

The last stanza of our theme hymn speaks about the results of God's saving grace in Christ. Those who have received God's grace by faith live in Christ who governs and directs their lives. He is not only the head of the church (Colossians 1:18), he is also the head of every Christian believer. We live in faith, trusting and obeying him, receiving the power of his Spirit, and pledging our loyalty to him. Because we live in this fashion, we know and feel our sins forgiven (stanza seven). We are confident that we belong to God and that God will care for us in every circumstance. We do not fear his wrath but humbly call ourselves God's children. This is what Wesley called assurance. It is reflected in hymns such as the following:

> *No condemnation now I dread,*
> > *Jesus, and all in him, is mine.*
> *Alive in him, my living head,*
> > *And clothed in righteousness divine,*
> *Bold I approach th'eternal throne,*
> *And claim the crown, through Christ my own.*
> > (A Collection of Hymns, #193)

A more detailed description of assurance is found in Wesley's hymn "How Can We Sinners Know":

> *How can we sinners know*
> *our sins on earth forgiven?*
> *How can my gracious Savior show*
> *my name inscribed in heaven?*
>
> *What we have felt and seen,*
> *with confidence we tell,*
> *and publish to the ends of earth*
> *the signs infallible.*
>
> *We who in Christ believe*
> *that he for us hath died,*
> *we all his unknown peace receive*
> *and feel his blood applied.*
>
> *We by his Spirit prove*
> *and know the things of God,*
> *the things which freely of his love*
> *he hath on us bestowed.*

The meek and lowly heart
that in our Savior was,
to us that Spirit doth impart
and signs us with his cross.

Our nature's turned, our mind
transformed in all its powers,
and both the witnesses are joined,
the Spirit of God with ours.
(A Collection of Hymns, #93, *altered*)

This hymn, especially the last stanza, speaks of "the witness of the Spirit" mentioned in Romans 8:14-17, in which Paul wrote about God's "Spirit bearing witness with our spirit that we are children of God." So, in Christ, we know and feel our sins forgiven. We are certain by God's Spirit at work in our lives that we belong to God whose loving care is foundation for our living.

All of this is an anticipation of heaven according to our theme hymn (stanza seven). God's grace experienced here is a foretaste of what awaits us in heaven. God's grace (love) for us is a participation in heaven while we are yet in this life. Our love for God and our neighbors is our living response and preparation for the life yet to come.

Questions for Reflection and Discussion

1. Why is it difficult for you to think of yourself as a sinner, as one who "misses the mark"?

2. What are the consequences of our sin against others and God?

3. In what ways are you aware of God's grace in your life?

4. What are appropriate responses to God's gracious love?

5. How are Charles Wesley's views on "assurance" helpful to you?

6. What does it mean to speak of Jesus as your Redeemer?

Chapter 2

The Triune God

1. *Maker [Father] in whom we live,*
   in whom we are and move,
   the glory, power, and praise receive
   for thy creating love.
   Let all the angel throng
   give thanks to God on high,
   while earth repeats the joyful song
   and echoes to the sky.

2. *Incarnate Deity,*
   let all the ransomed race
   render in thanks their lives to thee
   for thy redeeming grace.
   The grace to sinners showed
   ye heavenly choirs proclaim,
   and cry, "Salvation to our God,
   salvation to the Lamb!"

3. *Spirit of Holiness,*
   let all thy saints adore
   thy sacred energy, and bless
   thine heart-renewing power.
   Not angel tongues can tell
   thy love's ecstatic height,
   the glorious joy unspeakable,
   the beatific sight.

4. *Eternal, Triune God,*
   let all the hosts above,
   let all on earth below record
   and dwell upon they love.
   When heaven and earth are fled
   before thy glorious face,
   sing all the saints thy love hath made
   thine everlasting praise.

Christians around the world affirm faith in the Triune God. Whether Roman Catholic, Eastern Orthodox, or Protestant, this affirmation is central to our understanding of who God is and what God does. The Trinity is one of the essential beliefs of the Christian faith.

In 1784, John Wesley formulated twenty-four Articles of Religion, revised from the Thirty-nine Articles of the Church of England. He sent his revision to America to govern the beliefs of the people whom he had instructed to form a church they called the Methodist Episcopal Church. The first Article declared "Faith in the Holy Trinity" as follows:

> There is but one living and true God, everlasting, without body or parts, of infinite power, wisdom, and goodness; the maker and preserver of all things, both visible and invisible. And in unity of this Godhead there are three persons, of one substance, power, and eternity—the Father, the Son, and the Holy Ghost.

Countless hymns of Charles Wesley express faith in, and praise for, the Triune God, including the theme hymn of this chapter. Wesley's hymns on the Trinity are distributed throughout many hymnbooks that he and his brother John published during their ministries. Among them is the collection Charles published in 1767 titled *Hymns on the Trinity*, which includes 188 hymns on the Triune God.

Wesley was convinced that the church's historic doctrine of the Trinity was firmly grounded in the Bible and in the tradition of the church. As the early Christian church considered the biblical texts that described the nature of God, the identity of Jesus Christ, and the Holy Spirit whose presence was uniquely received on the Day of Pentecost (Acts 2), it concluded as the Articles of Religion state, God is one and exists in Three Persons: Father, Son, and Holy Spirit.

The church's traditional doctrine of the Trinity has been challenged often over the centuries and was vigorously disputed in

Wesley's time in the movement we know as Unitarianism. Although accepting the existence of God, the Unitarians, as their name implies, rejected a trinitarian understanding of God and repudiated the divinity of Christ, that is, that Jesus is the incarnation, or enfleshment, of God. Unitarianism remains organized today in North America as the Unitarian Universalist Association. Another religious group that finds trinitarianism unacceptable and describes itself as "antitrinitarian" is the Jehovah's Witnesses. They claim that the trinitarian understanding of God is not taught in the Bible. Other world faiths also find trinitarian teaching about God both troublesome and unacceptable. Nevertheless, the trinitarian understanding of God, one God in Three Persons, is basic Christian belief.

God the Father

Each of the first three stanzas of our theme hymn offers praise to one of the Three Persons of the Holy Trinity. The first stanza honors the Father, the second the Son, and the third the Holy Spirit.

Wesley had no difficulty referring to the First Person of the Trinity as Father. He believed that there is ample biblical evidence that this is a proper designation. In the Old Testament, God is called the parent of the Hebrew people and sometimes their Father (Deuteronomy 32:6). The New Testament also designates God as Father. Jesus frequently spoke of God as Father in various sayings and parables. He said that we should forgive others so that our "Father in heaven" may forgive us (Mark 11:25). The parable of the prodigal (Luke 15:11-32), which speaks about a father who waits patiently for his wayward son and who celebrates his return, is a story about God the Father who anticipates our coming back to him. Jesus' model prayer addressed God as, "Our Father in heaven" (Matthew 6:9; Luke 11:2). When he commissioned his closest followers to continue his ministry, Jesus said that they should make disciples of all people, "baptizing them in the name of the Father and of the Son and of the Holy Spirit" (Matthew 28:19). Several of the letters of the New Testament begin with a greeting of grace and peace, "from God our Father" (for example, Romans 1:7; 1 Thessalonians 1:1).

This "father" language for God raises questions for some persons. For example, if we call God "Father," must God be considered masculine? God is neither masculine nor feminine. God is personal, and God desires a personal relationship with each of us. Employing a term such as *father* protects belief in the personal God.

The term *Maker* is substituted for "Father" in our theme hymn. The problem for Wesleyan theology with making this change is that the whole Trinity, not simply the Father, possesses and exercises creating power, even though in this stanza it is primarily ascribed to the Father. In one place Wesley wrote:

> *Father, and Son, and Spirit join'd*
> *In the creating plan,*
> *Each is the Maker of mankind,*
> *And doth his work sustain.*
> (Hymns on the Trinity, #39)

In another hymn he wrote:

> *The Father, Son, and Holy Ghost,*
> *God in three Persons One,*
> *Created that celestial host,*
> *And made our earth alone.*
> (Hymns on the Trinity, #110)

To speak of the Father alone as the "Maker" was not satisfactory to Wesley, because it neglected the creative work of the other two Persons of the Trinity, Jesus and the Holy Spirit, who act with the Father in the task of creating.

"Father [Maker], in whom we live, in whom we are and move" is drawn directly from Acts 17:28 in which the writer quoted a passage from Paul's sermon in Athens: "For 'In [God] we live and move and have our being.'" This verse reminds us that God is the source of our life and that our existence is dependent on God.

Because of his creating love, the Father is worthy to receive "glory, power, and praise." Wesley's words are reminiscent of the book of Revelation, chapter 4, which describes the impressive scene in which the writer was transported to heaven. There he witnessed God seated on a throne surrounded by a heavenly host who sang:

> You are worthy, our Lord and God,
> to receive glory and honor and power,
> for you created all things,
> and by your will they existed and were created.
> (Revelation 4:11)

In both the Scripture passage and Wesley's hymn, we remember that we cannot give God glory or power, because they already belong to God. We can, however, acknowledge God's glory and power in worship and remember that we are living in God's presence.

Stanza one closes with a call to the heavenly company of angels and those on earth to unite in recognizing the majesty and power of God's creating love. Wesley was persuaded that there was an "angel throng," mostly because angels play an important role in the biblical story. *Angel* for the writers of the Bible meant "messenger of God." Angels appear in both Testaments, in which they are messengers of God's word and servants who do his work. Wesley exhorted them to "give thanks to God on high" who created and sustained them. He also entreated us humans on earth to enter into "joyful song" that "echoes to the sky." This joyous singing praises the Father who gives us life and who supports us by divine grace.

Jesus, God Incarnate

Stanza two of our theme hymn extols the Second Person of the Trinity, Jesus Christ, God Incarnate. Our attention is focused especially on the role of Jesus, whose atoning death opens the way for our salvation. Note that just as the whole Trinity, one God, engages in the work of creation, so the whole Trinity, one God, is the author of our salvation. It is God present in Jesus Christ through whom this salvation is accomplished.

Jesus, the "Incarnate Deity," is addressed as the one whose "redeeming grace" has liberated "all the ransomed race." We noted in the previous chapter that redemption in the ancient world referred to the process by which slaves were freed from bondage. In this stanza, redemption is emancipation from the domination and oppression of sin. It is also deliverance from the consequences of sin, from guilt and divine judgment. Grace, God's unearned forgiving and renewing love, releases us from sin's grip.

As the "ransomed race," Wesley bids us to offer thanks. Ransom is another important biblical concept and is similar to redemption. To ransom someone is to free the person from captivity. In the Old Testament, God is the One who ransoms the souls of people (Psalm 49:15). God rescues the people from their captivity, captivity not only to sin, but also to foreign powers: "And the ransomed of the

LORD shall return, / and come to Zion with singing; / everlasting joy shall be upon their heads; / they shall obtain joy and gladness, / and sorrow and sighing shall flee away" (Isaiah 35:10).

In the New Testament, God ransoms us through Jesus' death. Speaking of himself and his redemptive work, Jesus said, "For the Son of Man came not to be served but to serve, and to give his life as a ransom for many" (Mark 10:45). The earliest Christians understood themselves as people who had been ransomed by Jesus (1 Timothy 2:6). The writer of the book of Revelation spoke of Jesus as the one whose sacrifice had ransomed people of every sort in order that they might serve God (Revelation 5:9-10). Just as Wesley employed the biblical concept of redemption, he also used the biblical image of ransom to emphasize the achievement of God's emancipating grace in the death of Jesus.

For the grace that God has exhibited in the redeeming and ransoming work of Jesus, the "Incarnate Deity," all on earth and in heaven are called upon to offer thanks and praise. The "heavenly choir" about which Wesley spoke may include all those who have gone before us in the faith. This heavenly throng is composed of countless faithful persons, including our parents, grandparents, relatives, and friends who have received in faith God's redeeming grace in Jesus Christ. They are summoned to pay tribute to the God of grace by their exclamation, "Salvation to our God, salvation to the Lamb!" (see also Revelation 5:13).

Jesus is described as the Lamb in many Wesley hymns. In order to appreciate this title for Jesus we need to recall how important lambs are in the biblical narrative. Sheep were valuable animals in the ancient world. Clothing was made from their wool. When food was needed, they could be slaughtered. Most important, however, lambs were part of the sacrificial system, especially in making offerings to God on Passover and for the nation's sins on the annual Day of Atonement. The writers of the New Testament declared that the sacrificial system had been superseded by Jesus' sacrificial death on the cross. Several writers called Jesus "the Lamb," implying the sacrificial nature of his redeeming work (John 1:29; 1 Corinthians 5:7b; Revelation 5:12; 22:1). Wesley ended the second stanza with the heavenly choir singing, "Salvation to our God, salvation to the Lamb!"

God the Holy Spirit

The Third Person of the Trinity, the Holy Spirit, is called "Spirit of Holiness" in the third stanza of our theme hymn. This reference completes the naming of the Three Persons of the Triune God.

Jesus promised his followers that they would receive a fresh experience of God's Spirit following his resurrection that would empower them for their lives and ministry. Before his ascension, Jesus announced: "You will receive power when the Holy Spirit has come upon you; and you will be my witnesses in Jerusalem, in all Judea and Samaria, and to the ends of the earth" (Acts 1:8). This promise was fulfilled on the day of Pentecost (Acts 2).

The early Christians interpreted Pentecost not only as the realization of Jesus' promise, but also as the completion of the prophecy made in the Old Testament by the prophet Joel: "I will pour out my spirit on all flesh; / your sons and your daughters shall prophesy, / your old men shall dream dreams, / and your young men shall see visions" (Joel 2:28; Acts 2:17).

Always a methodical student of the Scripture, Charles Wesley understood the significance of Pentecost and the Holy Spirit for Jesus' followers. The Holy Spirit plays a prominent role in much of Wesley's hymnody. In 1746, he published a small hymnbook with thirty-two hymns for Whitsunday that he titled *Hymns of Petition and Thanksgiving for the Promise of the Father*. In these hymns, Wesley speaks of the Holy Spirit as the Spirit of grace, life, and divine power. The Spirit fills our souls with God's life and love.

The theme hymn of this chapter refers to the Holy Spirit as "sacred energy" who possesses "heart-renewing power" and whose dynamic presence constantly assures us that we belong to God. We are the "saints"—holy people by God's grace—mentioned in the second line of the third stanza ("let all thy saints adore"). The Spirit directs and encourages us to be the people God intends, supports and emboldens us in difficult situations, and empowers us to perform routine as well as remarkable acts in Jesus' name.

The Holy Spirit is given to individuals. Those who experience the enormous power and influence of the Spirit in their lives are filled with humility and joy. They know that they have not earned the favor of the Spirit's presence. It is freely given.

Although we offer praise for the overwhelming nature of God's grace made real in and through the Holy Spirit, our language cannot adequately express our joyful thanksgiving. Even "angel tongues" cannot summon sufficient jubilation to proclaim the "ecstatic heights" of God's marvelous love. By the Spirit's presence in us that inspires and nurtures holy living, we have a new vision of God, God's plan for us, and the place in the kingdom of heaven that awaits us. This "beatific sight" blesses us with confidence and joy.

The Holy Spirit is a gift not only to individuals but also to the church. Christian faith is personal but never private. Persons of faith always stand within the fellowship of people of faith, the Body of Christ, the church, and the Body of Christ in the church as they serve one another and the world around them. The church receives the Holy Spirit and the Spirit's gifts for its instruction, nurture, and mission.

Eternal, Triune God

The first three stanzas of our theme hymn offer praise and thanksgiving to each of the Three Persons of the trinitarian God. The final stanza recognizes that these are Three Persons of one God. They are not three separate gods. They are completely one in purpose, and they act absolutely in concert. Another Wesley hymn speaks of the Three Persons working as one in creation and redemption:

> *Hail Father, Son, and Spirit, great*
> *Before the birth of time,*
> *Enthron'd in everlasting state*
> *Jehovah Elohim!*
> *A mystical plurality*
> *We in the Godhead own,*
> *Adoring One in Persons Three,*
> *And Three in Nature One.*
>
> *From Thee our being we receive*
> *The creatures of thy grace,*
> *And rais'd out of the earth we live*
> *To sing our Maker's praise:*
> *Thy powerful, wise, and loving mind*
> *Did our creation plan,*
> *And all the glorious Persons join'd*
> *To form thy fav'rite, man.*

Again Thou didst, in council met,
Thy ruin'd work restore,
Establish'd in our first estate
To forfeit it no more:
And when we rise in love renew'd,
Our souls resemble Thee,
An image of the Triune God
To all eternity.
(Hymns on the Trinity, #87)

Wesley made no attempt to explain how one God can exist in Three Persons. He simply accepted it as a fact of Scripture, the faith of the church, and a mystery that reason strives to understand.

By the Father, and the Son,
And blessed Spirit made,
God in Persons Three we own,
And hang upon his aid:
Reason asks, how can it be?
But who by simple faith embrace,
We shall know the mystery,
And see Him face to face.
(Hymns on the Trinity, #124)

Reason was important for Wesley. He lived in the Age of Reason, the era that marked the beginning of modern science and philosophy. According to Wesley, reason must be valued. The mind is the gift of God that should be cultivated and used as all of God's gifts. Reason has limits, however. It cannot generate saving faith or create a holy life.

Right notions have their slender use,
But cannot a sound faith produce,
Or vital piety,
They cannot make the Godhead known,
Or manifest Jehovah One
In co-eternal Three.
(Hymns and Prayers to the Trinity, #28,
in Hymns on the Trinity)

Mystery has a prominent place in Wesley's hymns. He spoke about the presence and working of God's grace as a mystery. Jesus' death as a redeeming sacrifice is a mystery. Likewise, the triune nature of God is mysterious.

We teach the mystery
Of God both One and Three:
God himself both Three and One
Our divine commission seals,
Comes in attestation down,
In his church for ever dwells.
(Hymns on the Trinity, #134)

Our theme hymn closes with a recognition that "all the hosts above" and "all on earth below" acknowledge and dwell on the love of the Triune God for us and all creation, the love unmistakably exhibited and experienced in God's creation, redemption, and empowerment. In every circumstance, in heaven and on earth, all God's saints, God's holy people, sing everlasting praise for the demonstrated love of the Triune God.

Many hymns penned by Wesley echo praise for the Holy Trinity. Here is one of them:

We lift our hearts to Thee,
Jehovah on thy throne,
Co-equal, Co-eternal Three
In will and nature One:
With all the sons of grace
We in thy worship join,
Plurality of Persons praise,
And Unity Divine.

The Father made of none
We bow our souls before,
And Christ his uncreated Son
With equal zeal adore:
Transcending human thought
Jehovah's Self is He,
Incomprehensibly begot
From all eternity.

God, very God indeed
The Holy Ghost, we know,
From Son and Father did proceed,
And life on man bestow:
With Son and Father Him
Alike we glorify,
Jehovah, the true God, supreme
O'er all in earth and sky.

22

This glorious Trinity
We worship evermore:
None less, or greater of the Three,
None after or afore:
The Persons Three are One;
And who by faith embrace,
We soon on his triumphant throne
Shall see Him face to face.
(Hymns and Prayers to the Trinity, #1,
in Hymns on the Trinity)

In the following chapters we will pay special attention to the Second and Third Persons of the Trinity.

Questions for Reflection and Discussion

1. How do Wesley's hymns about the Trinity help us understand that the God we worship and serve is Three Persons in One?

2. How are creation and salvation (redemption) the work of all Three Persons of the Triune God?

3. Have you or someone you know experienced problems with speaking about God as Father? Why?

4. In what ways may we offer praise to the Triune God?

5. What roles do reason and mystery play in your faith?

Chapter 3

Jesus, God Incarnate

1. Hark! the herald angels sing,
   "Glory to the new-born King;
   peace on earth, and mercy mild,
   God and sinners reconciled!"
   Joyful, all ye nations rise,
   join the triumph of the skies;
   with th'angelic host proclaim,
   "Christ is born in Bethlehem!"
   Hark! the herald angels sing,
   "Glory to the new-born King!"

2. Christ, by highest heaven adored;
   Christ, the everlasting Lord;
   late in time behold him come,
   offspring of a virgin's womb.
   Veiled in flesh the Godhead see;
   hail th'incarnate Deity,
   pleased with us in flesh to dwell,
   Jesus, our Emmanuel.
   Hark! the herald angels sing,
   "Glory to the new-born King!"

3. Hail the heaven-born Prince of Peace!
   Hail the Sun of Righteousness!
   Light and life to all he brings,
   risen with healing in his wings.
   Mild he lays his glory by,

born that we no more may die,
born to raise us from the earth,
born to give us second birth.
Hark! the herald angels sing,
"Glory to the new-born King!"

This hymn has become one of the most popular Christmas carols celebrating the birth of Jesus. When it was first published in 1739, it was designated "Hymn for Christmas Day." Although we usually sing only the three stanzas printed above, the hymn originally had five, the first of which began with the words, "Hark, how all the welkin rings!" In the language of the eighteenth century, "welkin" referred to the heavens. So, the original first line of the hymn might have read, "Hark, how all the heavens ring!" to hail the birth of Jesus, God's Incarnate Word. George Whitefield, one of the principal leaders of the eighteenth-century evangelical revival in England and America, is credited with changing the first line to read, "Hark! the herald angels sing!" in his collection of hymns published in 1754.

Each stanza of the hymn is packed with scriptural and theological content. How often we sing it without giving to the text the attention it deserves. We will examine each stanza in order.

Jesus: Our Prophet, Priest, and King

The first stanza of our theme hymn begins with an invitation to listen to the "herald angels," the heavenly company of God's messengers who announced the birth of Jesus, the "new-born King." All on earth are summoned to listen to the glad proclamation that God has come among us in Jesus. A familiar passage from the Gospel of Luke in which the birth of Jesus is declared to the shepherds by "an angel of the Lord" forms the basis for this opening line. The angel said to them, "Do not be afraid; for see—I am bringing you good news of great joy for all the people: to you is born this day in the city of David a Savior, who is the Messiah, the Lord" (Luke 2:10-11). The Gospel writer then describes "a multitude of the heavenly host" praising God and saying, "Glory to God in the highest heaven, / and on earth peace among those whom he favors" (Luke 2:14).

Who was this Jesus born in Bethlehem? Both the biblical text and the hymn answer that question. He was the "new-born King," a title derived from the Old Testament, in which God is understood as the ruler not only of the Hebrew people, but also of all the earth (Psalm 10:16; 24:7-10; 47:7; 89:18). This royal title is also applied to Jesus in the New Testament, indicating his unity with God (1 Timothy 6:15; Revelation 17:14). Nathaniel, one of Jesus' twelve disciples, addressed him saying, "Rabbi, you are the Son of God! You are the King of Israel!" (John 1:49). At Christmas and throughout the year, we pause to exalt Jesus, our King.

In other hymns Charles Wesley spoke of Jesus not only as King, but also as Prophet and Priest.

> *Prophet, to me reveal*
> *Thy Father's perfect will:*
> *Never mortal spake like thee,*
> *Human prophet like divine;*
> *Loud and strong their voices be,*
> *Small, and still, and inward thine!*
>
> *On thee my Priest I call,*
> *Thy blood atoned for all:*
> *Still the Lamb as slain appears,*
> *Still thou stand'st before the throne,*
> *Ever off'ring up my prayers,*
> *These presenting with thy own.*
>
> *Jesu, thou art my King,*
> *From thee my strength I bring:*
> *Shadowed by thy mighty hand,*
> *Savior, who shall pluck me thence?*
> *Faith supports, by faith I stand,*
> *Strong as thy omnipotence.*
> (A Collection of Hymns, #186)

As Prophet, Jesus stands in the line of the great prophets who spoke on behalf of God (Matthew 16:14; Mark 6:15). Yet, no prophet spoke as he did. He not only delivered God's word, but also was the enfleshment of God's Word (John 1:14). Jesus, the Prophet, fully disclosed God and revealed God's will.

As Priest, Jesus has offered the complete and final atoning sacrifice for human sin that supplanted the sacrificial system of ancient Israel (Hebrews 7:27; 1 Corinthians 15:3-4). Through our acceptance and trust in Jesus' atoning death, we are reconciled to God.

Whereas, in our disobedience, we were counted enemies of God, through Jesus we become God's children. As King, Jesus is the ruler of our lives, to whom all in heaven and on earth bow in awesome obedience (Philippians 2:10-11). He is our Prophet, Priest, and King.

The good news of Jesus, the new-born King, stirs joy in all nations and peoples. "Joyful, all ye nations rise, join the triumph of the skies." Much of the news in our lives does not provoke joy and gladness. It is not difficult for international, national, and personal crises to overwhelm us. Too frequently good news is sparse. This hymn declares good news and lifts our spirits. It reminds us of God's unfailing presence and grace uniquely and fully known in the birth of Jesus about whom we sing, "Glory to the new-born King."

Veiled in Flesh

Several themes appear in the second stanza of our hymn. "Christ, the everlasting Lord" is dearly loved and adored by those in heaven. In the superb first chapter of the letter to the Hebrews, the writer talks about God's speaking to us by a Son. When the Son came into the world, God said, "Let all [the] angels worship him" (Hebrews 1:6). This command is echoed in the hymn as Christ is praised by those in heaven as "the everlasting Lord."

The birth of Jesus came "late in time." We can only appreciate this when we remember that the people of Israel expected the Christ, the Messiah, God's anointed one, to appear for many generations. The "long-expected" Jesus has now been born, "offspring of a virgin's womb" (Matthew 1:23). Charles Wesley wrote a wonderful hymn that Christians sing during the Advent season. That hymn, "Come, Thou Long-expected Jesus," speaks about the expectation of the Messiah's appearance and prays for Jesus to be born anew in our lives and in our world.

> *Come, Thou long-expected Jesus,*
>   *Born to set thy people free,*
> *From our Fears and Sins release us,*
>   *Let us find our rest in Thee:*
> *Israel's Strength and Consolation,*
>   *Hope of all the Earth Thou art,*
> *Dear Desire of every Nation,*
>   *Joy of every longing heart.*

Born thy People to deliver,
　Born a Child and yet a King;
Born to reign in Us for ever,
　Now thy gracious Kingdom bring;
By thine own eternal Spirit
　Rule in all our Hearts alone,
By thine all-sufficient Merit
　Raise us to thy glorious Throne.
(Hymns for the Nativity of Our Lord, #10)

The latter half of our theme hymn's second stanza speaks about a fact that Wesley emphasized frequently in his hymns—the incarnation, or enfleshment, of God in a human being. "Veiled in flesh the Godhead see; hail th'incarnate Deity." It must have been an extraordinary experience for Joseph and the shepherds in their fields near Bethlehem to be told by angels that the infant Jesus was the long-expected Messiah, the Lord, Emmanuel; that is, "God with us" (Matthew 1:23; Luke 2:11).

The earliest Christian community struggled with how to determine whether Jesus was God or a human being or both. If he was God, how could he be genuinely human? If he was human, how could he be God?

One group in the early church decided to solve this dilemma by denying Jesus' divinity. They rejected the virgin birth of Jesus, affirming that he was simply the human son of Mary and Joseph. As a man, they believed, Jesus perfectly fulfilled the Jewish law and was adopted by God as the messianic prophet. The adoption occurred when the Holy Spirit descended on Jesus in the form of a dove at his baptism (Matthew 3:13-17).

Another faction held the opposite position. They denied Jesus' humanity in order to assert his divinity. They believed that if Jesus was divine, he could not be human since divinity and humanity cannot mix. He only appeared to be human. So, they claimed, Jesus did not really suffer or die since only humans can suffer and die. He only "appeared" to suffer and die.

Rejecting both of these views, the early Christian church came to a consensus that Jesus was fully human and fully divine. It was convinced that this position was supported by biblical evidence (for example, John 1:1, 14; 1 John 4:2-3). Thus, both of the principal creeds of the church, the Apostles' Creed and especially the Nicene

Creed, affirm the complete humanity and divinity of Jesus. Wesley stated this truth when he spoke of Jesus as God "veiled in flesh" and "the incarnate Deity."

Many Charles Wesley hymns emphasize both the humanity and divinity of Jesus. Some are found in his *Hymns on the Trinity* (1767), including the following:

> *Very man, and very God,*
> *Thou hast bought us with thy blood:*
> *Two distinguished natures we*
> *In thy single Person see,*
> *God and man in thee alone*
> *Mix inseparably One.*
>
> *How could God for sinners die?*
> *How could Man the pardon buy?*
> *When thy human nature bled,*
> *Then the blood Divine was shed,*
> *Blood of Him who was in Thee*
> *God from all eternity.*
> (Hymns on the Trinity, #54)

How Jesus could be both human and divine is a reality that defies reason. Like so many other facets of the Christian faith, this mystery is to be accepted in faith with joy and thanksgiving.

Prince of Peace

Our theme hymn continues with a greeting of the birth of Jesus with jubilant praise: "Hail the heaven-born Prince of Peace!" *Peace* is one of the most important words in the Bible. The Hebrew word *shalom* (peace) is often used as a greeting or as a word of blessing when departing from someone and expresses a wish for harmony, prosperity, and well-being until meeting again. The Old Testament prophet Isaiah wrote about the promised Messiah whose name would be "Prince of Peace" (Isaiah 9:6).

"Peace" also appears in the New Testament in a variety of contexts. Many of the letters in the New Testament begin with the words *grace* and *peace* (1 Corinthians 1:3). Peace can mean a reconciled relationship with God whereby we are no longer enemies of

God who refuse to acknowledge him, resist his will, and stand under his judgment (Romans 5:1). It can also refer to harmonious relationships with other persons and nations and especially relationships within the church (Ephesians 4:1-3). Peace is the deeply personal experience of calm and assurance that results from knowing that God's presence, love, and protection are always present (Romans 15:13). Jesus is the "Prince of Peace" who brings this harmony and well-being to our lives. Peace is also the compatibility that God wishes in communities and among nations. Those who follow Jesus are invited to be a blessing to others as his peacemakers (Matthew 5:9).

"Hail the Sun of Righteousness! Light and life to all he brings, risen with healing in his wings." Wesley's words are rooted in the Old Testament prophet Malachi: "But for you who revere my name the sun of righteousness shall rise, with healing in its wings" (Malachi 4:2). Warning the people that God's severe judgment would fall on them for their evil deeds and lack of faith, Malachi announced the rising of "the sun of righteousness," which conveys healing and new life to those who remain humble, faithful, and obedient to God. Wesley claimed that Malachi's prophecy had been fulfilled in the birth of Jesus who brings "light and life" to all who acknowledge and follow him as the "new-born King."

The last half of the third stanza begins by speaking of Jesus setting his glory aside to become a man to dwell among us. This theme appears in the New Testament in the letter to the Philippians in which the writer states:

> Let the same mind be in you that was in Christ Jesus,
> who, though he was in the form of God,
> did not regard equality with God
> as something to be exploited,
> but emptied himself,
> taking the form of a slave,
> being born in human likeness.
> And being found in human form,
> he humbled himself
> and became obedient to the point of death—
> even death on a cross. (Philippians 2:5-8)

Wesley's use of Jesus' self-emptying, or laying aside his glory, is a prominent theme in several of his hymns. Here is a stanza from one of them that is a commentary on the Philippians passage:

Equal with God most high,
He laid his glory by:
He th'eternal God was born,
  Man with men he deigned t'appear,
Object of his creature's scorn,
  Pleased a servant's form to wear.
              (A Collection of Hymns, #187)

A more familiar example is one of the stanzas of the hymn "And Can It Be" that reads:

He left his Father's throne above
  (So free, so infinite his grace!),
Emptied himself of all but love,
  And bled for Adam's helpless race.
'Tis mercy all, immense and free,
For, O my God, it found out me!
              (A Collection of Hymns, #193)

Jesus left the majesty he possessed in heaven as one of the Three Persons of the Triune God to become a human being; to live like a human being; to suffer and die in our place; and to be raised as the Lord of Glory, King of Kings, and Lord of Lords. He did so in order that we might not die, but be raised as he has been raised. He did so in order that we might be given "second birth" by the pardoning grace of God.

Although the last two stanzas of the original hymn are not found in most modern hymnals, they are important expressions of the joy of Jesus' birth. They speak about the new life God has made possible in Jesus through whom sin in us is overcome, God's nature joined to ours, and the image of God restored in us.

Come, Desire of Nations, come,
Fix in Us thy humble Home,
Rise, the Woman's Conqu'ring Seed,
Bruise in Us the Serpent's Head.

Now display thy saving Pow'r,
Ruin'd Nature now restore,
Now in Mystic Union join
Thine to Ours, and Ours to Thine.

Adam's Likeness, Lord, efface,
Stamp thy Image in its Place,
Second Adam from above,
Reinstate us in thy Love.

Let us Thee, tho' lost, regain,
Thee, the Life, the Inner Man:
O! to All Thyself impart,
Form'd in each Believing Heart.
(Hymns and Sacred Poems,
"Hymn for Christmas Day")

In the midst of our celebrations of Christmas with carol-singing, family gatherings, gift-giving, and delicious feasts, we must never forget the One whose birth we commemorate at Christmas and throughout the year, the presence of God among us in Jesus Christ.

Questions for Reflection and Discussion

1. What do we know about God through the birth of Jesus?

2. What does it mean to you to call Jesus "Prophet, Priest, and King"?

3. "Risen with healing in his wings"—what healing does Jesus bring to our lives?

4. Is it reasonable to believe that Jesus is "the incarnate Deity," the enfleshment of God? Why or why not?

5. How should we relate to people who do not believe what we believe about Jesus?

6. How does Jesus bring "peace on earth"?

Chapter 4

The Holy Spirit

1. *Spirit of faith, come down,*
   Reveal the things of God,
   And make to us the Godhead known,
   And witness with the blood:
   'Tis thine the blood to apply,
   And give us eyes to see,
   Who did for every sinner die
   Hath surely died for me.

2. *No [one] can truly say*
   That Jesus is the Lord
   Unless thou take the veil away,
   And breathe the living word;
   Then, only then we feel
   Our interest in his blood,
   And cry with joy unspeakable,
   Thou art my Lord, my God!

3. *O that the world might know*
   The all-atoning Lamb!
   Spirit of faith, descend, and show
   The virtue of his name;
   The grace which all may find,
   The saving power impart,
   And testify to all [humankind],
   And speak in every heart!

4. Inspire the living faith
(Which whosoe're [receive],
The witness in [themselves they have],
And consciously [believe]),
The faith that conquers all,
And doth the mountain move,
And saves whoe're on Jesus call,
And perfects them in love.

The trinitarian God was at the center of Charles Wesley's under-standing of the Christian faith and life. He believed that one God in Three Persons—Father, Son, and Holy Spirit—accomplished the complete work of creation and salvation. Our theme hymn demon-strates Wesley's understanding of the Spirit's place in our faith.

The presence and influence of God's Spirit is prominent in the Bible. In the Old Testament the Spirit is sent forth by God (Genesis 1:2) and is God's breath in creation (Genesis 2:7; Psalm 33:6). The Spirit was a guide and inspiration for leaders and prophets (Numbers 11:25; Judges 3:10; Micah 3:8). A fresh experience of the Spirit is promised in Joel 2:28-32, in which the prophet announces: "Then afterward I [God] will pour out my spirit on all flesh." The early Christian community was convinced that God's promise had been fulfilled. They believed that Jesus' birth and baptism were events in which the Holy Spirit was an influential presence (Matthew 1:18; Mark 1:10). At the opening of his ministry, Jesus announced that the Spirit of the Lord had anointed him for his ministry (Luke 4:18). The early church also believed that God's promise of a unique and fresh outpouring of the Spirit was fulfilled on the day of Pentecost (Acts 2). Thereafter, all Christians were blessed in new ways by the presence of the Spirit and the Spirit's gifts.

Sunday, May 21, 1738, marked Charles Wesley's "personal Pentecost." After considerable spiritual self-examination and strug-gle, he surrendered to the redemptive power of God, claimed Christ as his Savior, and rejoiced in the presence and power of the Holy Spirit.

Many of Wesley's hymns celebrate the presence and role of the Holy Spirit. Among them is the small collection of thirty-two hymns for Whitsunday (Pentecost) that he published in 1746, entitled *Hymns of Petition and Thanksgiving for the Promise of the Father.* These hymns contain a wealth of biblical and theological content further disclosing his understanding of the person and work of the Holy Spirit for the Christian and the church.

Revealer and Leader

The first stanza of our theme hymn, "Spirit of faith, come down," sets the tone for the hymn. It is a prayer to the Holy Spirit, the "Spirit of faith," to perform God's work among us. Wesley strongly affirmed the biblical reality of the Holy Spirit as a person, the Third Person of the trinitarian God. Therefore, the Holy Spirit should not be referred to impersonally as "it," but as a Person, one who is in total union with the Father and the Son and who works in concert with them.

Central to the Spirit's work is revelation. The apostle Paul spoke of the role of the Holy Spirit in revealing who God is, what God does for our salvation, and the gifts God offers through the Spirit to enrich human life. He wrote that "these things God has revealed to us through the [Holy] Spirit" (1 Corinthians 2:10).

Revelation by the Holy Spirit awakens our spiritual senses in several ways. First, it is through the Holy Spirit that we know the "Godhead," that is, one God whom we acknowledge in Three Persons. The Three Persons of the Godhead acted in perfect unity as one God to create the universe and all that is in it, including the human race. One God in Three Persons also accomplished salvation for us. Our hymns, liturgy, and prayers testify to the Godhead, one God in Three Persons.

Second, the Holy Spirit is a "witness with the blood." "Blood" refers to the saving work of Jesus in his death on the cross. His saving sacrifice is often referred to in the New Testament as "the blood of Christ" (1 Corinthians 10:16; Ephesians 2:13; 1 Peter 1:19). Wesley affirmed that the Holy Spirit testifies to the redemptive and reconciling work of Jesus as our High Priest who has sacrificially offered his life for our salvation. The Spirit reveals the saving work of God in Jesus, the Savior whose sacrifice makes our salvation possible. The Spirit is also instrumental in making salvation real in us. In applying Jesus' blood to us, the Spirit is as much a participant in our salvation as the Father and the Son. Revealing God's plan of salvation is the first stage of the Spirit's work. Administering God's gracious pardon achieved through the shedding of Jesus' blood is the second dimension of the Spirit's work.

The first stanza of our theme hymn closes with asking the Holy Spirit to help us see and understand that Jesus has died for everyone. We ask to be given "eyes to see" that he "did for every sinner die" (compare Deuteronomy 29:4 where Moses says that God has not yet given the people "eyes to see"). Wesley was thoroughly convinced by his study of the Bible that God intended salvation and new life for all (John 3:16; Romans 5:8). God's grace is present in all people and enables them to respond to the offer of salvation, reconciliation, and new life in Jesus' sacrificial death. All who respond in faith receive the divine gift of forgiveness and renewal. Another hymn attributed to Charles, appended to John Wesley's sermon "Free Grace," resonates with the truth that God's saving grace is accessible to all.

> For every *man [Christ] tasted death,*
>   He *suffered once for* all,
> He *calls as many souls as breathe,*
>   And all *may hear the call.*
>
> A *power to choose, a will to obey,*
>   Freely *his grace restores;*
> We all *may find the Living Way,*
>   And call the Savior ours.
>
> . . . .
>
> He *would that* all *his truths should own,*
>   His *gospel all embrace,*
> Be *justified by faith alone,*
>   And *freely saved by grace.*
> *("Free Grace," 1739, selected stanzas, emphasis added)*

The Holy Spirit is asked to reveal not only that Jesus died for all, but also that he "died for me." God's saving work in Christ is for all, but that also means that it is personal—for me!

Breathing New Life

Our theme hymn's second stanza opens with the exclamation that, "No one can truly say that Jesus is the Lord" except through the influence of the Holy Spirit (1 Corinthians 12:3). Removing the veil of unbelief (2 Corinthians 3:16) and breathing into us God's living Word, the Holy Spirit enables us to accept God's gift of new life.

"Jesus is Lord" may have been the first creed, or statement of belief, in the Christian church. In the Old Testament, "LORD" appears frequently as one of the names of God (Psalm 33:1, 39:12; Isaiah 53:1; Jeremiah 9:23-24). In many places in the New Testament, Jesus is called Lord (Romans 10:9; 1 Thessalonians 1:3). A classic passage is found in the letter to the Philippians in which Paul speaks of Jesus' obedience in giving up his life on the cross:

> Therefore God also highly exalted him
>   and gave him the name
>   that is above every name,
> so that at the name of Jesus
>   every knee should bend,
>   in heaven and on earth and under the earth,
> and every tongue should confess
>   that Jesus Christ is Lord,
>   to the glory of God the Father. (Philippians 2:9-11)

What does it mean to say that Jesus Christ is Lord? Wesley believed it was more than a verbal act. Jesus' lordship signifies that he has sovereign authority over one's life. Jesus rules one's thinking, speaking, and acting. He controls one's relationships with others, behavior at home and work, spending habits, the care of one's body, and every other facet of one's life. Jesus is the Master of all that one is and all that one has. We are never alone in life. The Holy Spirit is our constant companion, encouraging and empowering us to accept God's love demonstrated in Jesus and to submit to Jesus as the center of our lives.

When Wesley continued, "Then, only then, we feel our interest in his blood," he was echoing the words of the writer of the New Testament letter to the Ephesians: "In [Jesus Christ] we have redemption through his blood, the forgiveness of our trespasses, according to the riches of his grace that he lavished on us" (Ephesians 1:7-8*a*). Our privilege to receive pardon and new life is based on God's grace manifested in the life, death, and resurrection of Jesus. This right is something we experience.

Charles Wesley's hymns often spoke of feeling God's presence and salvation. He believed that true religion is a matter of the heart as well as of the mind. It is a matter of feeling as well as of thinking. God's presence and grace are not simply to be described but experienced. So, he wrote:

What we have felt and seen,
With confidence we tell,
And publish to the sons of men
The signs infallible.

We who in Christ believe,
That he for us hath died,
We all his unknown peace receive,
And feel his blood applied.
(A Collection of Hymns, #93,
selected stanzas, emphasis added)

What is our response to the goodness of God through the saving work of Jesus that is infused into our lives by the Holy Spirit? We are prompted to address Jesus with indescribable joy in the words of the hymn: "Thou art my Lord, my God!" This statement is undoubtedly based on the exclamation of the apostle Thomas, whose doubt about Jesus' resurrection caused him to say that he would not believe until he actually touched the risen Christ. When Jesus appeared again to the disciples with Thomas among them, he invited Thomas to touch his wounds and said, "Do not doubt but believe." Thomas replied, "My Lord and my God!" (John 20:27-28). In a similar manner, the Holy Spirit leads us to know and feel that Jesus' sacrifice makes possible our forgiveness and reconciliation with God. Following the Spirit's guidance, we affirm Jesus' person and redemptive work as divine work. He is our Lord and God.

Holy Spirit and Universal Grace

Stanza three of our hymn resonates with a theme comparable to the first stanza. The redemption God has designed is offered to everyone, to the whole world. The stanza begins with a prayer that the world might know Jesus Christ, "the all-atoning Lamb." Jesus is called the Lamb in several places in the New Testament. John the Baptist, pointing to Jesus, is reported to have said, "Here is the Lamb of God who takes away the sin of the world!" (John 1:29). Jesus is also described as the Lamb in many places in the book of Revelation (for example, Revelation 5:6, 12-13; 21:14, 22). This title for Jesus is directly related to the Old Testament temple system of sacrifice for which a lamb was slain as an atonement for the sins of the people. The early Christians held that the practice of temple sacrifice has been replaced forever by the sacrificial death of Christ, the Lamb of God.

To speak of Jesus as "the all-atoning Lamb" attests two facts. First, Jesus' sacrifice covers all sin. No sin is excluded from the atoning death of Jesus. Second, his sacrifice is an atonement for all people. To put it in Wesley's words, it is atonement for "the world." It heals the relationship between God and human beings that has been damaged by our disobedience, failure to acknowledge his claim on our lives, and refusal to worship him. To know the all-atoning Lamb, Jesus Christ, is to acknowledge him as Lord and God, to trust him as our Savior, and to obey him in all things.

When Wesley spoke of the Holy Spirit descending to show "the virtue of his name," he was referring to the powerful name of Jesus. We recall again that in biblical times someone's name was more than a label of identification. One's name was a distinguishing mark that actually represented the nature of a person, the essence of who a person was and what that person did. We can see this in the name of the Savior. Jesus, from the Hebrew name *Yeshua* (meaning "God saves"), is the name of the One whom Christians call their Redeemer and Lord. Jesus' name represents the salvation he accomplished for us, especially in his sacrificial death. Wesley's prayer was that the Holy Spirit would show the powerful redemption available to all in Jesus.

The Spirit possesses the power to impart, or convey, to all people God's forgiveness, reconciliation, and new life made possible in the sacrificial death of Jesus. The truth of God's universal grace is mentioned in one of the lesser-known letters in the New Testament:

> For the grace of God has appeared, bringing salvation to all, training us to renounce impiety and worldly passions, and in the present age to live lives that are self-controlled, upright, and godly, while we wait for the blessed hope and the manifestation of the glory of our great God and Savior, Jesus Christ. He it is who gave himself for us that he might redeem us from all iniquity and purify for himself a people of his own who are zealous for good deeds. (Titus 2:11-14)

If, as Wesley believed, the Holy Spirit imparts the saving power of God's grace, then it is obvious why the stanza ends with the plea that the Spirit "testify to all [humankind], and speak in every heart."

As we might suspect, the earlier version of this hymn had the words, "testify to mankind." Wesley, of course, thought salvation encompassed all, both men and women. The use of *humankind* more accurately carries Wesley's intent.

God's universal grace is emphasized again as there is an appeal to the Holy Spirit to speak to the whole human race. This is underscored by the use of "every sinner," that "the world might know," "all may find," and "speak in every heart." This emphasis is characteristic of Wesleyan Methodism. Both John and Charles Wesley believed it to be a central truth of the Bible and Christian tradition. In sermons, tracts, correspondence, hymns, and by every other means at their disposal, they proclaimed the message that the salvation of the Triune God is offered to everyone. God's grace is at work in everyone, and by that grace all are free to respond to God.

Living Faith and Assurance

The hymn's final stanza opens with an appeal that the Holy Spirit "inspire the living faith" in us and all people. *Inspire,* a term not frequently used in the Bible, literally means "to breathe into." God's Spirit breathing into human beings is a concept that is present in various places in Scripture. God's "breath of life" activated human life (Genesis 2:7). The dry bones in the valley described in Ezekiel come to life as God breathes into them (Ezekiel 37:1-14). Jesus breathed on his disciples, and they received the Holy Spirit to prepare and empower them for their ministry in his name (John 20:22-23).

Wesley spoke about the "living faith" that includes the act of having faith, that is, trusting in God's steadfast love and all that accompanies it. It is likely that he was also talking about *the* faith, that is, what he considered the body of belief essential to Christianity. This includes belief in the Triune God (Father, Son, and Holy Spirit), the seriousness of human sin, the sacrificial death and resurrection of Jesus, the healing and pardoning grace of God through Christ, and the response of those who follow Christ in leading a holy life. This "living faith" is breathed into us by the Holy Spirit. It is God's gift available to all of us.

Those who receive this gift of the Spirit knowingly believe. They are steadfast in faith, holding on by conviction and in confidence. Their trust is in God, and they receive the witness of God's Spirit. The

Holy Spirit bears witness with our spirit that we are God's children (Romans 8:16). The Wesleyan tradition has held that we can be sure of our standing before God by the witness of the Holy Spirit. We do not have to wonder about our status with God. John Wesley wrote:

> The testimony of the [Holy] Spirit is an inward impression on the soul, whereby the Spirit of God directly "witnesses to my spirit that I am a child of God"; that Jesus Christ hath loved me, and given himself for me; that all my sins are blotted out, and I, even I, am reconciled to God. ("The Witness of the Spirit, I," 1746)

Charles Wesley raised the question of assurance and the witness of the Spirit in some of his hymns:

> *We by his Spirit prove*
> *And know the things of God;*
> *The things which freely of his love*
> *He hath on us bestowed:*
> *His Spirit to us he gave,*
> *And dwells in us, we know;*
> *The witness in ourselves we have,*
> *And all his fruits we show.*
>
> *The meek and lowly heart,*
> *That in our Saviour was,*
> *To us his Spirit does impart,*
> *And signs us with his cross:*
> *Our nature's turned, our mind*
> *Transformed in all its powers;*
> *And both the witnesses are joined,*
> *The Spirit of God with ours.*
> (A Collection of Hymns, #93)

A stanza of Wesley's well-known hymn "And Can It Be" also speaks about the confident assurance of Christ's people:

> *No condemnation now I dread,*
> *Jesus, and all in him, is mine.*
> *Alive in him, my living head,*
> *And clothed in righteousness divine,*
> *Bold I approach th'eternal throne,*
> *And claim the crown, through Christ my own.*
> (A Collection of Hymns, #193)

The faith that the Holy Spirit breathes into us, according to Wesley, conquers all and is able to move mountains. Jesus spoke about having faith so as to move mountains (Mark 11:23), and Paul wrote about having such faith (1 Corinthians 13:2). Removing mountains was a common Jewish phrase that meant trusting God's grace to assist with eliminating all of life's difficulties, even the most burdensome.

The stanza closes with a comment that those who are pardoned and given new life call on Jesus' name (Acts 2:21). He is our Savior and Lord. We must remember, however, Jesus' warning that simply calling on him is insufficient. He said, "Not everyone who says to me, 'Lord, Lord,' will enter the kingdom of heaven, but only the one who does the will of my Father in heaven" (Matthew 7:21). So, evidence of Jesus' lordship is given in both our words and acts.

Building to a climax in the final stanza, Wesley stated that the Spirit-inspired faith about which we sing aims at sanctification, holiness, and perfection in love. Christian perfection is a central theme in the Wesleyan understanding of Christian faith. It is the ultimate goal for us of the Triune God's salvation made possible by divine grace, especially through the crucifixion and resurrection of Jesus. Christian perfection is nothing less than being filled with love for God and for our neighbors. The focus of our faith is the God who "perfects [us] in love."

Questions for Reflection and Discussion

1. How does Wesley's hymn help you understand the role of the Holy Spirit in the Christian faith and life?

2. What does it mean to say that Jesus is Lord?

3. What is the "saving power" about which Wesley spoke in stanza three?

4. Wesley spoke of faith perfecting us in love. What does that mean to you?

5. How do you experience the "witness" of the Holy Spirit (mentioned in stanza four) in your life?

Chapter 5

The Christian Life

1. Love divine, all loves excelling,
    Joy of heaven, to earth come down,
   Fix in us thy humble dwelling,
       All thy faithful mercies crown!
   Jesus, thou art all compassion,
       Pure, unbounded love thou art;
   Visit us with thy salvation!
       Enter every trembling heart.

2. Breathe, O breathe thy loving Spirit
       Into every troubled breast!
   Let us all in thee inherit;
       Let us find that second rest.
   Take away our bent to sinning;
       Alpha and Omega be;
   End of faith, as its beginning,
       Set our hearts at liberty.

3. Come, Almighty to deliver,
       Let us all thy grace receive;
   Suddenly return, and never,
       Never more thy temples leave.
   Thee we would be always blessing,
       Serve thee as thy hosts above,
   Pray, and praise thee without ceasing,
       Glory in thy perfect love.

> *4. Finish then thy new creation,*
> *Pure and spotless let us be;*
> *Let us see thy great salvation*
> *Perfectly restored in thee;*
> *Changed from glory into glory,*
> *Till in heaven we take our place,*
> *Till we cast our crowns before thee,*
> *Lost in wonder, love, and praise.*

Among Charles Wesley's best-known hymns, this hymn is found in the hymnals and songbooks of many denominations. It imitates John Dryden's patriotic poem, "Fairest Isle, all isles excelling," found in Henry Purcell's opera "King Arthur" (1691). In comparison to Dryden's poem, Wesley's text seeks to praise not a nation, but the God who is above all national loyalties. He speaks about the God who is love and who calls people to love him and one another.

The clear scriptural basis for the hymn is 1 John 4:7-12:

> Beloved, let us love one another, because love is from God; everyone who loves is born of God and knows God. Whoever does not love does not know God, for God is love. God's love was revealed among us in this way: God sent his only Son into the world so that we might live through him. In this is love, not that we loved God but that he loved us and sent his Son to be the atoning sacrifice for our sins. Beloved, since God loved us so much, we also ought to love one another. No one has ever seen God; if we love one another, God lives in us, and his love is perfected in us.

Love Divine: God's Nature and Name

Our theme hymn opens with offering praise to God, who is named "Love divine" and who has come among us in the person of Jesus Christ, incarnate love, "joy of heaven, to earth come down." In another hymn, based on the story of Jacob wrestling with an angel (Genesis 32:24-32), Wesley explored the nature and name of God. Rather than dwelling on Jacob's struggle with the angel, he brings us into this Old Testament story as travelers who are seeking to know the One whose love for us is unexcelled.

Come, O thou Traveller unknown,
* Whom still I hold, but cannot see!*
My company before is gone,
* And I am left alone with thee;*
With thee all night I mean to stay,
And wrestle till the break of day.

I need not tell thee who I am,
* My misery or sin declare;*
Thyself hast called me by my name,
* Look on thy hands and read it there.*
But who, I ask thee, who art thou?
Tell me thy name, and tell me now.

. . . .

Yield to me now—for I am weak,
* But confident in self-despair!*
Speak to my heart, in blessings speak,
* Be conquered by my instant prayer:*
Speak, or thou never hence shalt move,
And tell me if thy name is LOVE.

'Tis Love! 'Tis Love! Thou diedst for me;
* I hear thy whisper in my heart.*
The morning breaks, the shadows flee,
* Pure Universal Love thou art:*
To me, to all, thy mercies move—
Thy nature, and thy name, is LOVE.
    (A Collection of Hymns, #136, *altered*)

After praising God as "Love divine" in our theme hymn, Wesley leads us to pray that God will secure his loving presence in us since we are meant to be God's humble dwelling place. Isaiah spoke of God's dwelling "with those who are contrite and humble in spirit, / to revive the spirit of the humble, / and to revive the heart of the contrite" (Isaiah 57:15). The emphasis on God's presence is more intimate in Wesley's words. God dwells not only *with* us, but in us. We recall Paul's words that we are God's temple, the humble place in which God's Spirit dwells (1 Corinthians 3:16). This indwelling love is crowned with God's faithful goodwill and kindness.

We know about the nature and depth of God's love through its incarnation in Jesus. His compassionate ministry of teaching and healing (for example, Matthew 9:36) and his sacrificial death on the cross (John 3:16) demonstrate the depth and breadth of divine mercy and reveal God's love for us as "pure, unbounded." Can anyone imagine or expect more than divine boundless love!

The stanza closes with asking God in Christ to come to us with grace that forgives, transforms, empowers, and renews our relationship with God as well as our associations with our families, friends, and the whole human community. Like the refreshing rain that falls on parched ground, God's presence and loving-kindness are always available to fortify and enliven us for any worrying ("trembling") circumstance.

"Inspired" by God

The second stanza of our theme hymn begins as a prayer for inspiration. We have seen in another chapter that the term *inspire* literally means "to breathe into." "Breathe, O breathe thy loving Spirit" entreats God to breathe into us, to inspire us with the Holy Spirit. We ask this not only for ourselves, but also for every troubled person. Is there anyone who is not troubled by something or someone? We live daily with problems and distress of various kinds—feelings of unworthiness, guilt, betrayal, threats, insecurity, failure, health, and anxiety about the future—to name just a few. Others' troubles, especially those whom we deeply love, are also matters about which we care. Concern for their welfare has a great influence on us. In this hymn we pray for others in trouble as well as for ourselves.

Like all of us, Charles Wesley knew firsthand the hardships and adversity of life—a horrible disease that almost killed his wife and left her permanently scarred, the death of their young son, persecution by fellow clergy and mobs, serious disagreements with his brother John, the demise of his parents, and countless other problems. His prayer was that God's sustaining, loving Spirit breathe into him in the midst of life's trials. The distress and suffering of others also moved him, as a devoted Christian and loving pastor, to pray that God's Spirit breathe into them as well. God's Spirit is available to all, and genuine Christian faith seeks the blessings the Spirit brings to us and others.

Two illustrations of Wesley's concern for people in extremely troubled situations exhibit not only his prayer that God breathe into them, but also his openness to be a means by which the Spirit might act through his words and deeds.

Following in the footsteps of Jesus, Wesley was concerned for the poor. He spoke about them as his "best friends," stayed in their homes, and preached to and prayed for them. After suffering a severe leg injury that left him in pain and exhausted, he reported that the poor "laid [him] on their bed, the best they had" and cared for him (Journal, August 10, 1745). It is not surprising that his hymns recognized the plight of the poor, voiced God's love for them, and spoke of his resolve to employ his gifts in ministry for them. In one hymn, Wesley prayed for the mind of Christ to guide him as he provided for the poor out of his own substance:

> *Thy mind throughout my life be shown,*
> *While, listening to the sufferer's cry,*
> *The widow's and the orphan's groan,*
> *On mercy's wings I swiftly fly,*
> *The poor and helpless to relieve,*
> *My life, my all, for them to give.*
> (Hymns and Psalms, #318)

The second illustration concerns Wesley's compassion for prisoners. Throughout their ministries, both Charles and his brother John showed great sympathy for those in prison. Inmates were among the most despised people of their day. The Wesleys visited prisoners (Matthew 25:36), prayed for them, accompanied to the gallows those who were to be executed, and in other ways ministered to them. Charles wrote a number of hymns for prisoners, especially for those facing execution, including this one:

> *O Savior of sinners distress'd,*
> *The sighs of Thy captive attend,*
> *And succour, and set him at rest,*
> *And ransom his soul to the end:*
> *Our brother, whose burden we bear,*
> *Whom into Thy hands we resign,*
> *Preserve with Thy tendrest care,*
> *And seal him eternally Thine.*
> (Journal of Charles Wesley, Vol. II, 460-61)

Christ's people cannot neglect the needs of others, including the needs of the most desperate. Their prayers that God comfort the troubled are always accompanied by their willingness to have God use their words, deeds, and gifts to provide solace and support to those in need.

Those who seek to be filled with God's Spirit are prompted to ask for other blessings, enumerated in the rest of the second stanza.

(1) We ask to "inherit" the gifts of God's grace and to find the "second rest." At several places in the New Testament, Christians are said to inherit blessings made possible by God's grace in Christ (for example, Ephesians 1:11, 14; Hebrews 9:15). They discover life's fullest joy as God's children who are inhabited by the Spirit. Furthermore, in God's presence, those who have been troubled by life and who have persevered in grace find "the second rest" (Hebrews 4:1-11), peace with God, themselves, and the world.

(2) "Inspired" by the Spirit, we petition God to remove our "bent to sinning." This is a critical request. Since the Wesleys believed that we are always free to obey or disobey God and are inclined willfully to rebel against God (Romans 2:23; 7:18-20), we ask God to eradicate the tendency to sin in us. As we allow God to uproot our inclination to sin, by grace we become more and more conformed to be the people God intends, receptive to God's love, and full of love for God and one another.

(3) We call on God to be the "Alpha and Omega" of our lives. Alpha and omega are the first and last letters of the Greek alphabet. The writer of the book of Revelation spoke of God as the "Alpha and Omega" (Revelation 1:8; 21:6; 22:13), the One who is the beginning and end of all things. Here Wesley speaks of God as the One who is the creator of faith as well as its goal. We ask God to be first and last in our lives.

(4) Finally, we entreat God to "set [our] hearts at liberty." The biblical writers emphasize deliverance, freedom, and liberty for God's people. The questions are always two: (a) Freedom or liberty *from* what? (b) Freedom or liberty *to* what? We seek liberation from the guilt and power of sin. Conversely, we ask for freedom to think, speak, and act in accordance with God's will, the way that leads to the fullest and best life.

Blessing God

The plea for God's presence and action in our lives continues in the third stanza of our theme hymn. God is addressed as the

"Almighty," a name for God found frequently in the Old Testament (Genesis 17:1; Ruth 1:20; Isaiah 13:6), although not as often in the New Testament (2 Corinthians 6:18; Revelation 1:8; 16:7). In both Testaments, the Almighty can accomplish whatever he pleases, especially in the deliverance of his people. God can deliver us from any circumstance that threatens us as persons or as a community. As the Almighty, God's plan cannot finally be thwarted or defeated.

"Let us all thy grace receive." Since the very nature of God is love, we are asking to receive the fullness of God's presence as divine love and all that accompanies it. That includes pardon, healing, comfort, encouragement, sensitivity, goodness, and strength, among other gifts. It means being more and more conformed to the image of God (Genesis 1:27), that is, by divine grace living with and for God.

Our prayer is that God's mighty delivering and transforming presence become a reality now and never leave us. In Wesley's words, "suddenly return, and never, never more thy temples leave." The temples about which we sing may be interpreted in at least two ways. First, as Paul pointed out, we are personally the temples of God (1 Corinthians 3:16-17). God dwells in each of us as persons who follow Christ and cultivates gifts in our lives to enrich our faith and discipleship. Second, as the Temple in Jerusalem, destroyed many centuries ago, was a place for the faithful community to gather for worship, the temples of God's presence today are not exclusively personal. They are also the communities in which we gather to worship and serve him.

The stanza closes with a pledge of response to the Holy One, the trinitarian God, who comes to us and whose life we receive. It is God whom "we would be always blessing," whom alone we would exalt. Wesley mentioned three ways that can be accomplished.

(1) We would serve God as the hosts above. Such serving is to put our whole selves at God's disposal, all that we are and all that we have. As the "host of heaven" (1 Kings 22:19; Nehemiah 9:6; Luke 2:13) are constantly present with God to enjoy God's presence and to offer their service to God, we, too, present ourselves to be used in any way God chooses (Romans 12:1). This includes serving our neighbors since, as Jesus said, we meet God in our neighbor's need (Matthew 25:31-46). We bless God through serving.

(2) Ceaseless prayer and praising blesses God. The Wesleyan tradition has always recognized the necessity of prayer and praise. John

Wesley spoke of prayer as one of the principal "means of grace," a gift by which God brings faith to maturity. It was no less so for Charles. Wesleyan people not only say our prayers; we also sing them. Charles Wesley's hymns provide countless texts that lift prayer and praise to God. Praise of God is not only offered in word and music, however. It is also offered in what we do with the talents and opportunities God gives each and all of us. We bless God through prayer and praise.

(3) We glory in God's perfect love. Much of what we call love does not possess the quality of perfection. It lacks depth and faithfulness. We suffer betrayal, rejection, and pain from those who say they love us. Regrettably, our love for others displays the same deficiencies. It is not perfect love. This is not so with God's love for us. God's love is boundless and steadfast. It is love that continues even when it is crucified, absorbing all the hurt and pain and remaining constant in every circumstance. Christian faith and life is rooted in God's perfect love and prompts us to be faithful and steadfast in our love for God and others.

Pure and Spotless Love

Our theme hymn reaches its conclusion with a prayer that God complete the new creation in us. How often this stanza is sung without paying proper attention to the significance and meaning of its opening words: "Finish then thy new creation, / pure and spotless let us be."

Paul declared: "If anyone is in Christ, there is a new creation: everything old has passed away; see, everything has become new!" (2 Corinthians 5:17). He continued by saying that all of this is the gift of God's grace (verse 18). According to Wesley, the new creation, accepting God's pardoning and justifying grace in Jesus, begins with the new birth (John 3:1-8) and continues to mature in a life of holiness and love—love for God and love for our neighbor (which includes everyone!).

Charles Wesley believed that the new creation of perfect love, purity, and spotlessness is not finalized until the time of one's death. Then, God's salvation will result in the perfect restoration of God's image in each of us. In the meantime, through the work of divine grace, Christians pray for and seek to be increasingly conformed to the mind of Christ (Philippians 2:5). Wesley affirmed that God's salvation has been "perfectly restored" in the work of the trinitarian God. In a sermon copied from his brother but approved and preached by him on several occasions, Charles described this restoration in the following way. It is:

> to re-exchange the image of Satan for the image of God, bondage for freedom, sickness for health. Our one great business is to raise out of our souls the likeness of our destroyer, and to be born again, to be formed anew after the likeness of our Creator. It is our one concern to shake off this servile yoke and to regain our native freedom; to throw off every chain, every passion and desire that does not suit an angelical nature. The one work we have to do is to return from the gates of death to perfect soundness; to have our diseases cured, our wounds healed, and our uncleanness done away. ("The One Thing Needful," I:5)

The idea of being changed and, thereby, restored to the image of God continues in our hymn as Wesley speaks of our being "changed from glory into glory." This echoes the words of Paul: "All of us, with unveiled faces, seeing the glory of the Lord as though reflected in a mirror, are being *transformed into the same image from one degree of glory to another;* for this comes from the Lord, the Spirit" (2 Corinthians 3:18; emphasis added). This process continues until we take our place in heaven. Wesley was not preoccupied with speaking about heaven. He understood, however, that the ultimate goal of the faithful is the place God has prepared for them when this life has run its course (John 14:1-3).

When we "take our place" in the heavenly kingdom, prepared for us by God and made possible by Jesus' atoning death and resurrection, we surrender all power and authority to God before whom we "cast our crowns"—signs of authority—as did the twenty-four elders in the book of Revelation (Revelation 4:10). Like them, we offer obedience and adoration.

In these circumstances at the end of this life and at the beginning of the next, we find ourselves "lost in wonder, love, and praise." We confess the wonder and the mystery of God's nature, creative power, and grace shown to us, the unworthy. Accepting the overwhelming love of God for each and all of us, we respond by loving God and the whole company of those in whose fellowship we now dwell and those yet to join us. We are wholly committed to, and absorbed by, love. We exalt the One who has given us life and new life through the Son.

Another Wesley hymn text, not as popular as the theme hymn of this chapter, includes many of the emphases found in it and speaks about the Christian life in a typically Wesleyan manner:

> *Plead we thus for faith alone,*
> *Faith which by our works is shown;*
> *God it is who justifies,*
> *Only faith the grace applies,*
> *Active faith that lives within,*
> *Conquers earth, and hell, and sin,*
> *Sanctifies, and makes us whole,*
> *Forms the Savior in the soul.*
>
> *Let us for this faith contend,*
> *Sure salvation is its end;*
> *Heaven already is begun,*
> *Everlasting life is won.*
> *Only let us persevere*
> *Till we see our Lord appear;*
> *Never from the rock remove,*
> *Saved by faith which works by love.*
> (A Collection of Hymns, #507)

The Christian life, created, nurtured, and molded by the Triune God, is always characterized by faith that works by love—a maturing love for God and for others.

Questions for Reflection and Discussion

1. How does "Love divine" excel and transform all other forms of love?

2. When have you experienced the "inspiration" of God?

3. How can we demonstrate care for the poor and for the prisoners?

4. In what ways do you and your church "bless" God?

5. What is "pure and spotless" love? How can it be attained?

6. How would you describe "faith that works by love"?

Chapter 6

Christian Community: The Church

1. *Christ, from whom all blessings flow,*
   Perfecting the saints below,
   Hear us, who thy nature share,
   Who thy mystic body are.

2. *Join us, in one spirit join,*
   Let us still receive of thine;
   Still for more on thee we call,
   Thou who fillest all in all.

   . . . .

3. *Move, and actuate, and guide,*
   Diverse gifts to each divide;
   Placed according to thy will,
   Let us all our work fulfill.

4. *Never from thy service move,*
   Needful to each other prove;
   Use the grace on each bestowed,
   Tempered by the art of God.

   . . . .

5. *Many are we now, and one,*
   We who Jesus have put on;
   There is neither bond nor free,
   Male nor female, Lord, in thee!

6. Love, like death, hath all destroyed,
Rendered our distinctions void!
Names, and sects, and parties fall,
Thou, O Christ, art all in all!

Biblical faith is personal, but it is not solitary. By God's grace, every person is free to embrace the creating, forgiving, and renewing love of God. Then each of us is called to join others in the journey of worship, fellowship, and ministry in the name of the Triune God. Christian people, as the ancient Hebrews, find strength, encouragement, and direction in the community of faith created and sustained by God. For Christians, that community is the church. John and Charles Wesley believed that the church was formed by God to be a blessing to its members and, through its members, a blessing to the world. We cannot be Christians in solitude.

Grounded in the New Testament letter to the Ephesians and other important biblical passages, our theme hymn speaks about the nature of the church, the necessity for its unity, the ministry to which it is called, and the gifts that equip it to do God's will. The writer of Ephesians wrote:

> I therefore, the prisoner in the Lord, beg you to lead a life worthy of the calling to which you have been called, with all humility and gentleness, with patience, bearing with one another in love, making every effort to maintain the unity of the Spirit in the bond of peace. There is one body and one Spirit, just as you were called to the one hope of your calling, one Lord, one faith, one baptism, one God and Father of all, who is above all and through all and in all. But each of us was given grace according to the measure of Christ's gift. . . . The gifts he gave were that some would be apostles, some prophets, some evangelists, some pastors and teachers, to equip the saints for the work of ministry, for building up the body of Christ, until all of us come to the unity of the faith and of the knowledge of the Son of God, to maturity, to the measure of the full stature of Christ. (Ephesians 4:1-7, 11-13)

Our theme hymn was originally published in 1740 in a collection written by John and Charles Wesley titled *Hymns and Sacred Poems.* It appeared in a lengthy section designated "The Communion of Saints." That section began with an address to the Triune God, stressing the unity of the Three Persons of the Trinity: Father, Son, and Holy Spirit. The unity of God is the basis for the solidarity of the Christian community, the church.

Christ's Mystic Body

The opening stanza addresses Jesus Christ "from whom all blessings flow." In contrast to praising the trinitarian God, as in the familiar congregational hymn "Praise God from Whom All Blessings Flow," Jesus, the Second Person of the Trinity is called on as the One whose gracious presence and favor brings us, "the saints below," to maturing love for God and one another. This is a recognition that Christ assists his people to "holiness of heart and life," a principal theme of Wesleyan theology. He accomplishes this through the presence and gifts of his Spirit, the Holy Spirit, who guides, encourages, and nurtures the Christian community and every person who belongs to it.

In prayerful language, we who bear the name of Christ and who share his life and nature (2 Peter 1:4) ask him to hear us. What is Christ's "nature" that we share? We remember Wesley's hymn "Come, O Thou Traveler Unknown," which deals with the question of God's name and nature. In that hymn, Wesley plainly says that the "nature and name" of God is love (1 John 4:8, 16). To share the nature of Christ is to know the love of God in one's life and to be moved to love God and others (1 John 4:7-12).

Those who share the nature of Christ, who are his people, are his "mystic body." One of the prominent images for the church in the New Testament is the body of Christ (Ephesians 1:22-23; Colossians 1:18). This imagery was used by Paul to underscore the close relationship that exists between Christ and his people (Romans 12:5; 1 Corinthians 12:12). It is also employed to proclaim that Christ's body, the church, is composed of many members but depends on and is guided by Christ, its head (Ephesians 5:23; Colossians 1:18). Christ is the church's sovereign source of unity, direction, and purpose.

Wesley was never hesitant to use the terms *mystery* and *mystic* in his hymns. Convinced that reason was a gift of God to be received gratefully and used faithfully, as we have observed elsewhere, Wesley was equally persuaded that reason has its limits. Human reason is incapable of understanding certain aspects of the Christian faith. Among these are how God can be Three Persons in One, the manner in which Jesus' death can be an atonement for sin, and the way in which the sacraments can convey God's grace to the recipient. In the last portion of the first stanza of our theme hymn, which speaks of the church as Christ's "mystic body," Wesley voices wonder at the mystery that the church is considered the "body of Christ." In another hymn, he describes the earliest church as a "mystic fellowship of love" (*A Collection of Hymns*, #16).

Unity in Diversity

Our prayer hymn continues by asking Jesus to join together all those who are members of his community, the church. We may recall Jesus' prayer in John 17 in which he prayed for the unity of his disciples. It reads in part: "As you, Father, are in me and I am in you, may they also be in us, so that the world may believe that you have sent me. The glory that you have given me I have given them, *so that they may be one, as we are one, I in them and you in me, that they may become completely one*, so that the world may know that you have sent me and have loved them even as you have loved me" (John 17:21*b*-23; emphasis added).

The Christian church is characterized by diversity. We are male and female. Some are wealthy. Others, in poverty, struggle daily to find adequate food, clothing, and shelter. Our educational backgrounds differ and our vocations are varied. There are racial differences. We come from a variety of nations around the world. In some places Christians are a majority. In others we are a tiny part of the population. Christians live in security in many places, while in others they are persecuted for their faith. Yet, amidst the wide diversity of Christ's people, a diversity that often may be considered a gift, something transcends our dissimilarities. Our unity in Christ overshadows our differences and forms the basis for the community of those who are bound to him and to one another (Galatians 3:28).

As Christ's people, we receive the benefits of his life, death, and resurrection, and the presence of the Holy Spirit, who is the gift of the Father and the Son. He gives us tasks to perform as well as the means by which to accomplish them. We have received his presence, gifts, and blessing. Yet we realize that there is more he wishes us to receive and do. Therefore, we call on him and open our lives to him, ready to do with our lives what he wishes. Christ is the one who fills us and the church with his presence and gifts. He fills "all in all" (Ephesians 1:23).

Gifted by God

A fresh experience of God's Spirit, the Holy Spirit promised by Jesus, was given to the Christian community on the day of Pentecost (Acts 2). The Holy Spirit inspired, guided, fortified, and energized the church to proclaim the good news of God's love in word and deed and equipped it to meet opposition and persecution. The same Spirit remains among us as we seek to do God's will and to fulfill Christ's ministry in our time. Stanza three of our theme hymn, therefore, opens with a plea that Christ's Spirit activate and lead the community and its members.

God not only favors us with the presence of the Spirit, but also blesses us with the Spirit's diverse gifts. These are the *charismata*, a Greek word that means "the free gifts of God's grace." This Greek word forms the basis for our English word *charismatic*, often used to describe a gifted person. God's free gifts are diverse. They are mentioned in many places in the Bible (for example, 1 Corinthians 12:4-11). Wesley referred to the variety of gifts given to the members of the community. He wrote, "diverse gifts to each divide."

Although Wesley did not speak about the significance of God's gifts, there are at least four reasons why they are given. (1) God gives them to help us remember that each of us is important to God. (2) They are critical in building and strengthening our faith and witness. (3) The gifts not only nurture our personal faith, but also enhance the life and ministry of the Christian community as each member uses them for the sake of others. (4) When the gifts are received, and faithfully developed and employed, they bring honor to God through whose grace they are given.

Although some today speak about a "charismatic movement" in the church and members of that movement refer to themselves as "charismatics," it is important to remember that all Christians are charismatic. All Christ's people receive free gifts of God's grace, though the gifts may vary widely from person to person (Romans 12:6; 1 Corinthians 12:4). Someone may have the gift of teaching, another the gift of preaching, and another the gift of leading. All of us are given the gift of giving to and serving others. These gifts are given according to God's will and enable God to fulfill his will in the world.

Called to Serve

As individuals and members of the body of Christ, the church, we are called into God's service (Luke 4:8; Ephesians 6:7). We are equipped for serving by the gifts that God freely gives to each one of us. We offer our service in countless ways. In some circumstances, the service God commissions may not be demanding and may bring us happiness and satisfaction. Teaching in the church school, ushering, preparing the elements for the Lord's Supper, or sharing in the leadership of worship may bring us great pleasure. Volunteering at a hospital, a clothing bank, or a soup kitchen provides other means of offering ourselves and our gifts to God. Furthermore, we must never forget that we serve God in familiar places, where we work, with our families, and with those who live next door.

God may call us to serve in other situations that are difficult, painful, or risky, however. Caring for the seriously ill, supporting an unpopular position on a social issue, or giving financial support to those in need when our own finances are precarious, are examples of these more demanding ways of serving. Moreover, Christians in some parts of the world worship and serve God in the face of severe opposition and even persecution. They suffer discrimination and physical abuse simply because they are Christ's people. Since they are our brothers and sisters, we suffer in their suffering.

We not only offer service to God as individuals, but also use our talents and gifts effectively in the fellowship of other Christians. "Needful" of one another, we realize that there are some situations in which we can do together what we can never do as individuals. In the body of Christ, the church, we furnish one another encouragement, assistance, and support. The "grace on each bestowed" and the gifts given to each are joined and exercised in the Christian community, the church, to bring about God's purpose in the world.

Wesley closed the fourth stanza of our hymn with a striking phrase, "tempered by the art of God." The service to which we are called, personally and jointly in the fellowship of the church, and the grace-gifts that equip us for serving are fashioned, integrated, and strengthened by God to fulfill his design for us and all creation. We and our gifts are "tempered by the art of God."

Many, yet One

Stanza five begins with the affirmation, "Many are we now, and one." The Christian church is composed of many millions of people around the world. They represent a wide diversity of nations, races, and languages. They differ in gender, class, educational background, and theological views and in many other ways. In spite of multiple differences, different gifts, and being called into various ministries, we are bound together by faith in, and loyalty to, Jesus Christ. Paul reminds us that we have "put on" Jesus Christ (Romans 13:14; Galatians 3:27). Christ's name was initially put on us at our baptism, and, by God's grace, our faithful allegiance and devotion to him continually deepens. In our Bible study, prayer, worship, reception of the Lord's Supper, and ministry to others in the company of Christ's people, we continue to "put on" Christ. We, who are many, are one body in Christ (1 Corinthians 10:17).

The New Testament writers underscored the unity in diversity of the Christian community. This can be seen as early as the book of Acts in which the Christian community is described as displaying increasing inclusiveness. Women and men meet together for nurture and worship (Acts 1:14). The gospel is preached to Samaritans, to an Ethiopian eunuch, and to Gentiles, as well as to Jews (Acts 8:5, 26-39; 10). It is God's will that the community be united with God and that its members understand, recognize, and prize their common relationship in Christ. Wesley closed the stanza by affirming unity in Christ: "there is neither bond nor free, male nor female, Lord, in thee!" This declaration is rooted in Paul's words in his letter to the Galatians:

> For in Christ Jesus you are all children of God through faith. As many of you as were baptized into Christ have clothed yourselves with Christ. There is no longer Jew or Greek, there is no longer slave or free, there is no longer male and female; for all of you are one in Christ Jesus. (3:26-28)

God's love surpasses the bounds of gender, nationality, language, race, and class. Authentic Christian community, imitating God's love for all people, embraces Christ's people in a fellowship of worship and service characterized by faith working by love.

Christ All in All

Emphasis on the unity of the church reaches its highest point in the final stanza of our theme hymn. Wesley began with an unusual comparison of love to death. We know what death can do. It destroys life and separates us from those we love. In Wesley's language, on the one hand, death "renders all distinctions void." Love, on the other hand, creates and nurtures life. Yet, like death, it possesses the power to overwhelm the distinctions that keep us from knowing and appreciating others. Love brings us together. Since all of us are subject to physical death, which ultimately eradicates the differences among us—that is, we all die—genuine love overcomes all the distinctions that separate us from one another. This is compelling testimony to the strength of love! One of the Old Testament writers puts it, "love is strong as death" (Song of Solomon 8:6). While both love and death may level all human distinctions, we affirm that love is always stronger than death. We base this conclusion on the triumph of God's loving purpose in the resurrection of Jesus.

In a sweeping ecumenical statement, Wesley announced that when the Christian community is primarily informed by, and committed to, love, "names and sects and parties fall." To believe this is to see all Christian believers, regardless of their denominational affiliation or individual church, as members of Christ's "mystic body." Paul expressed this belief like this:

> Now I appeal to you, brothers and sisters, by the name of our Lord Jesus Christ, that all of you be in agreement and that there be no divisions among you, but that you be united in the same mind and the same purpose. For it has been reported to me by Chloe's people that there are quarrels among you, my brothers and sisters. What I mean is that each of you says, "I belong to Paul," or "I belong to Apollos," or "I belong to Cephas," or "I belong to Christ." Has Christ been divided? Was Paul crucified for you? Or were you baptized in the name of Paul? (1 Corinthians 1:10-13)

The writer of Ephesians spoke about the unity we have in Christ when he wrote, "There is one body and one Spirit, just as you were called to the one hope of your calling, one Lord, one faith, one baptism, one God and Father of all" (Ephesians 4:4-6).

The hymn ends with the declaration that Christ is the "all in all" (Colossians 1:15-20; 3:11). The writer of Ephesians echoed this conviction in a slightly different manner:

Speaking the truth in love, we must grow up in every way into him who is the head, into Christ, from whom the whole body, joined and knit together by every ligament with which it is equipped, as each part is working properly, promotes the body's growth in building itself up in love. (Ephesians 4:15-16)

The belief that Christ is "all in all" provides the context in which Christians live and minister. It is Christ from "whom all blessings flow," perfecting us in love for God, for one another, and for the whole world.

Questions for Reflection and Discussion

1. Why did God create the church? What role does the church have in your life?
2. What gifts has God given you, and how can they be used for personal growth and service in the world?
3. How is diversity in the church a blessing?
4. What does it mean to "put on" Jesus (stanza five)?
5. What do you think about Wesley's comparison of death to love in stanza six?
6. Wesley said that Christ is "all in all." What did he mean?

Chapter 7

The Lord's Supper

1. O the Depth of Love Divine,
    Th'Unfathomable Grace!
Who shall say how Bread and Wine
    God into [us] conveys!
How the Bread his Flesh imparts,
    How the Wine transmits his Blood,
Fills his Faithful People's Hearts
    With all the Life of God!

2. Let the wisest Mortal show
    How we the Grace receive:
Feeble Elements bestow
    A Power not theirs to give:
Who explains the Wondrous Way?
    How thro' these the Virtue came?
These the Virtue did convey,
    Yet still remain the same.

3. How can heavenly spirits rise
    By earthly Matter fed,
Drink herewith Divine Supplies
    And eat immortal Bread?
Ask the Father's Wisdom how;
    [Christ] that did the Means ordain
Angels round our Altars bow
    To search it out, in vain.

4. Sure and real is the Grace,
　The Manner be unknown;
　Only meet us in thy Ways
　And perfect us in One.
　Let us taste the heavenly Powers,
　　LORD, we ask for nothing more;
　Thine to bless, 'tis only Ours
　　To wonder, and adore.

From the earliest days of the church, Christians have gathered to initiate persons into the church through baptism and to celebrate the Lord's Supper. The Lord's Supper is also known as the Eucharist or Holy Communion. The Protestant Reformation of the sixteenth century declared baptism and the Lord's Supper to be the only sacraments of the church, although the Roman Catholic Church observed seven sacraments. To justify their claim, Protestants held that only two sacraments were initiated by Jesus to be continued among his people.

Baptism is administered only once in a person's life. The Lord's Supper, however, is received regularly by Christ's people. When John Wesley sent the Articles of Religion to America in 1784 to govern the life of American Methodists, he included Article XVIII, which reads in part:

> The Supper of the Lord is not only a sign of the love that Christians ought to have among themselves one to another, but rather is a sacrament of our redemption by Christ's death; insomuch that, to such as rightly, worthily, and with faith receive the same, the bread which we break is a partaking of the body of Christ; and likewise the cup of blessing is a partaking of the blood of Christ.

There are, of course, other "means of grace," gifts of God, which, when properly employed, nurture faith and holy living. Among these are prayer, reading and studying the Bible, and fasting. For Charles Wesley, however, no means of grace was more important than the Lord's Supper. Speaking of its superiority, he wrote:

The Prayer, the Fast, the Word conveys,
　When mixt with Faith, thy Life to me,
In all the Channels of thy Grace,
　I still have Fellowship with Thee,
But chiefly here my Soul is fed
With Fullness of Immortal Bread.
　　(Hymns on the Lord's Supper, #54)

Believing that the Lord's Supper is the principal means by which God's saving, confirming, and nurturing grace is conveyed to its recipients, John and Charles Wesley regularly received communion throughout their adult lives. Commenting in his sermon on Acts 20:7, which reads, "On the first day of the week, when we met to break bread," Charles stated that the Bible and the church's tradition make clear that Christians should receive communion at least weekly. Further evidence of his conviction of the importance of the Lord's Supper is the large number of hymns that reflect his understanding of the sacrament. In 1745, Wesley published 166 of them, including the theme hymn of this chapter, in *Hymns on the Lord's Supper*, a booklet still available in reprint.

Before examining the four stanzas of our theme hymn, it may be helpful to offer a brief overview of the Wesleyan understanding of the Lord's Supper. Holy Communion is viewed as being invaluable to Christians for at least three reasons.

First, the Lord's Supper is a memorial, a way of remembering (1 Corinthians 11:23-26), which sets before us the suffering and atoning death of Christ. As we come to the Lord's table to receive the bread and to drink from the cup, we remember that Christ died for us (Romans 5:8). The writers of the New Testament declared that there is no clearer evidence of God's love for us than the life, death, and resurrection of Jesus. We are reminded of that love when we commune.

> *Jesu, suffering Deity,*
> *Can we help remembering Thee,*
> *Thee, whose Blood for Us did flow,*
> *Thee, who [died] to save thy Foe!*
>
> *Thee Redeemer of Mankind,*
> *Gladly now we call to mind,*
> *Thankfully thy Grace approve,*
> *Take the Tokens of thy Love.*
> (Hymns on the Lord's Supper, #12)

Second, the Lord's Supper is an anticipation. Receiving the elements at the Lord's table, we look toward the future, to the consummation of the kingdom of God, when we will all enjoy the fullness of God's presence in joy and peace (Matthew 26:26-29). The Lord's Supper is an "antepast of heaven," a foretaste of the heavenly messianic feast at which all God's people will gather (Matthew 8:11) to delight in fellowship and to extol God's love.

> *Come let us join with one Accord*
> *Who share the Supper of the LORD,*
> > *Our LORD and Master's Praise to sing,*
> *Nourish'd on Earth with living Bread*
> *We now are at his Table fed,*
> > *But wait to see our Heavenly King;*
> *To see the great Invisible*
> *Without a Sacramental Veil,*
> > *With all his Robes of Glory on,*
> *In rapt'rous Joy and Love and Praise*
> *Him to behold with open Face,*
> > *High on his Everlasting Throne.*
>
> *The Wine which doth his Passion shew,*
> *We soon with Him shall drink it New*
> > *In yonder dazzling Courts above,*
> *Admitted to the Heavenly Feast*
> *We shall his choicest Blessings taste,*
> > *And banquet on his richest Love . . .*
> > *(Hymns on the Lord's Supper, #93)*

Third, the Lord's Supper is more than a memorial and an anticipation. God uses it as a means of conveying grace into the lives of those who receive it in faith. This third meaning is emphasized in our theme hymn.

Unfathomable Grace

The hymn opens with words of wonder and praise for the immeasurable breadth and depth of God's love for us and all creation (Ephesians 3:18-19). The awesome nature of this divine love is underscored by referring to it as "unfathomable grace." It is too immense to be measured and too mysterious to be comprehended fully (Romans 11:33). Every day, in countless ways, we encounter God's overwhelming grace. In this hymn, however, Wesley speaks especially about recognizing and experiencing divine presence and love in the Lord's Supper.

The opening exclamation about God's grace sets a tone for the remainder of the hymn, much of which echoes the mysterious nature of grace and the manner in which it is conveyed in the sacrament. Who can say how ordinary bread and wine become a channel through which God's presence and blessing are imparted to us! How can common bread convey his flesh, and wine transmit his blood (1 Corinthians 10:16)! These are not questions but exclamations. They are affirmations of the mysterious means God uses to strengthen our faith, support us in our need, and fortify us for ministry. Chosen and blessed by God, they are means by which God "fills his faithful people's hearts with all the life of God!" (Ephesians 3:18-19). If that is so, we should eagerly and humbly receive the Lord's Supper as frequently as possible.

We observed earlier in commenting on other hymns that Charles Wesley possessed a high regard for reason. Since our minds are one of God's great gifts to us, reason has a rightful place. It enables us to read and understand the Bible. Reason is used when we seek to understand God's nature, action, and will and when we relate faith to issues that confront us personally and socially. Reason has its limits, however, especially when it comes to matters of faith. By itself, reason cannot produce vital faith or generate appropriate Christian living. Reason alone cannot completely comprehend the triune nature of God or fully understand God's ways. While acknowledging the goodness and necessity of human reason, Wesley always allowed room for mystery. The manner in which Christ is present in the Lord's Supper is one of those grand mysteries.

Bread and Wine Convey God's Power

The theme of God's breathtaking mystery continues in the second stanza of our theme hymn. The "wisest mortals" struggle to explain the manner in which God's grace is given and received in Holy Communion as well as in God's other mysteries (Isaiah 55:8-9; 1 Corinthians 1:19-20).

Bread and wine were staple foods in the ancient world. They were used by Jesus in the upper room meal with his disciples before his arrest and crucifixion (Luke 22:14-20). Over the centuries, these two "elements," bread and wine, have been used by those who follow Jesus' instruction that they continue to observe this meal in remembrance of him (1 Corinthians 11:23-26). Although many churches continue to use wine in the celebration of Communion, others, under the influence of the nineteenth-century American temperance movement, have chosen to use unfermented grape juice rather than wine.

Charles Wesley claimed that in the Lord's Supper the "feeble elements" of bread and wine, ordinary and basic foods, are blessed by God to carry an extraordinary power ("virtue") not normally theirs. These two common elements convey the power of new life and holiness in a "wondrous way."

Although bread and wine convey power to transform and cultivate holiness in us, Wesley was insistent that the elements "remain the same." They do not become anything other than bread and wine. The Roman Catholic Church teaches that at a certain time in the liturgy of the mass, the elements of bread and wine mystically and substantially become the actual body and blood of Jesus, even though in appearance they remain bread and wine. This change is known as the miracle of transubstantiation. Protestants reject this interpretation. For Methodists, this matter is treated in the 1784 Articles of Religion sent to America by John Wesley: "Transubstantiation, or the change of the substance of bread and wine in the Supper of our Lord, cannot be proved by Holy Writ [the Bible]."

Mystery Ordained by Christ

Still considering the mysterious nature of the Lord's Supper, Wesley raised the question of how we can be spiritually renewed and uplifted by consuming "earthly matter," that is, bread and wine. Blessed by God, we drink "divine supplies and eat immortal bread." But how can this be?

Wesley advised that since we are puzzled by how God's grace is mediated through the communion elements, we "ask the Father's wisdom how: Christ who did the means ordain." He was simply affirming the New Testament Gospels and the writings of Paul that give a clear account of Jesus' institution of this means of grace:

For I received from the Lord what I also handed on to you, that the Lord Jesus on the night when he was betrayed took a loaf of bread, and when he had given thanks, he broke it and said, "This is my body that is for you. Do this in remembrance of me." In the same way he took the cup also, after supper, saying, "This cup is the new covenant in my blood. Do this, as often as you drink it, in remembrance of me." For as often as you eat this bread and drink the cup, you proclaim the Lord's death until he comes. (1 Corinthians 11:23-26)

To underscore the mystery of divine grace conveyed in ordinary elements, Wesley claimed that even the angels do not understand how this takes place.

Receiving God's grace through bread and wine in the Lord's Supper is a personal act, but it is more than something we do individually. Normally, we celebrate the Lord's Supper in the company of family and friends, brothers and sisters in Christ. Holy Communion is an act of worship that represents our unity in Christ here and anticipates our fellowship when we gather in heaven. Another of Wesley's hymns speaks of our oneness in Christ:

> How happy are thy Servants, LORD,
>> Who thus remember Thee!
> What Tongue can tell our sweet Accord,
>> Our perfect Harmony!
>
> Who thy Mysterious Supper share,
>> Here at thy Table fed,
> Many, and yet but One we are,
>> One undivided Bread.
>
> One with the Living Bread Divine,
>> Which now by Faith we eat,
> Our Hearts, and Minds, and Spirits join,
>> And all in JESUS meet.
>
> So dear the Tie where Souls agree
>> In Jesu's Dying Love;
> Then only can it closer be,
>> When all are join'd above.
>> (Hymns on the Lord's Supper, #165)

Real Grace in the Lord's Supper

The concluding stanza of our theme hymn reinforces belief that God's love is conveyed in the Lord's Supper to those who receive it in faith: "Sure and real is the grace." The mysterious nature of this conveyance is also reiterated: "the manner be unknown." The stanza then turns to a prayer that God meet us in whatever ways God chooses, the Lord's Supper being one of those ways. We pray to God that, by divine grace, we be perfected; that God's image be restored in us (2 Corinthians 3:18); and that we grow more and more into the likeness of Christ (Romans 8:29; Philippians 2:5). This is the goal of the Christian life—complete holiness of heart and life, which is, by God's grace, loving God with all that we are and have and loving our neighbor as ourselves.

We ask God to allow us to "taste the heavenly powers" as we receive his grace in Holy Communion. There is nothing more for which we ask than God's blessing. Joining with others in heaven and on earth, we are filled with wonder and adoration as we consider the grace made manifest to us in the Lord's Supper (Romans 11:33).

Although Wesley rejected the idea that the crucified and risen Christ is substantially present in the elements of bread and wine and rejected the notion that the Lord's Supper is merely a memorial meal in which the elements are only symbols of the crucified Lord, he believed that Jesus was truly spiritually present at the Lord's Supper. In at least two hymns he spoke of Jesus' "Real Presence" in the sacrament:

> *Great is thy Faithfulness and Love,*
> *Thine Ordinance can never prove*
> *Of none Effect and vain,*
> *Only do Thou my Heart prepare,*
> *To find thy Real Presence there,*
> *And all thy Fullness gain.*
> (Hymns on the Lord's Supper, #66)

> *We need not now go up to Heaven*
> *To bring the long-sought Saviour down,*
> *Thou art to All already given:*
> *Thou dost ev'n Now thy Banquet crown,*
> *To every faithful Soul appear,*
> *And shew thy Real Presence here.*
> (Hymns on the Lord's Supper, #116)

The Lord's Supper not only is a holy meal that fortifies our spiritual lives and binds us to Christ and one another; but also prepares us to do God's will in the world. Therefore, Wesley proposed this prayer to be sung after the Supper has been celebrated:

> *Take my Soul and Body's Powers,*
> *Take my Mem'ry, Mind, and Will.*
> *All my Goods, and all my Hours,*
> *All I know, and all I feel,*
> *All I think, and speak, and do;*
> *Take my Heart—but make it new.*
>
> *Now, O GOD, thine own I am,*
> *Now I give Thee back thy own,*
> *Freedom, Friends, and Health, and Fame,*
> *Consecrate to Thee alone;*
> *Thine I live, thrice happy I,*
> *Happier still, for Thine I die.*
>
> *FATHER, SON, and HOLY GHOST,*
> *One in Three, and Three in One,*
> *As by the celestial Host,*
> *Let thy Will on Earth be done;*
> *Praise by All to Thee be given,*
> *Glorious LORD of Earth and Heaven.*
> (Hymns on the Lord's Supper, #155)

Questions for Reflection and Discussion

1. How is the Lord's Supper important in your life?

2. How have your beliefs about the Lord's Supper changed over the years?

3. How do you believe God's grace is conveyed to those who faithfully receive the elements in the Lord's Supper?

4. How frequently should we receive the Lord's Supper?

5. When, if ever, have you been reluctant to receive Holy Communion?

6. In the fourth stanza of our theme hymn, Wesley speaks of God's perfecting us. What did he mean?

Chapter 8

Christ's Resurrection and Christian Hope

1. *Christ the Lord is risen today, Alleluia!*
   Earth and heaven in chorus say, Alleluia!
   Raise your joys and triumphs high, Alleluia!
   Sing, ye heavens, and earth reply, Alleluia!

2. *Love's redeeming work is done, Alleluia!*
   Fought the fight, the battle won, Alleluia!
   Death in vain forbids him rise, Alleluia!
   Christ has opened paradise, Alleluia!

3. *Lives again our glorious King, Alleluia!*
   Where, O death, is now thy sting? Alleluia!
   Once he died our souls to save, Alleluia!
   Where's thy victory, boasting grave? Alleluia!

4. *Soar we now where Christ has led, Alleluia!*
   Following our exalted Head, Alleluia!
   Made like him, like him we rise, Alleluia!
   Ours the cross, the grave, the skies, Alleluia!

5. *Hail the Lord of earth and heaven, Alleluia!*
   Praise to thee by both be given, Alleluia!
   Thee we greet triumphant now, Alleluia!
   Hail the Resurrection, thou, Alleluia!

6. King of glory, soul of bliss, Alleluia!
Everlasting life is this, Alleluia!
Thee to know, thy power to prove, Alleluia!
Thus to sing, and thus to love, Alleluia!

Although we usually sing this hymn on Easter, it is a song of rejoicing for the Christian throughout the year. Celebrating the victorious power of God over sin and death, these words express the indomitable hope of Christian life and witness. The event of Jesus' resurrection forms the confident foundation for the way we think, speak, and act. Combining the accounts of Jesus' resurrection in the Gospels (Matthew 28; Mark 16; Luke 24; John 20), Charles Wesley's words also remind us of Paul's emphasis on the resurrection in 1 Corinthians 15.

Originally titled "Hymn for Easter Day," this jubilant poem was first published in 1739 with eleven stanzas. It has undergone editorial changes over the years, but its substance has not been altered. References to Jesus' resurrection appear in many of Wesley's hymns. As evidence of the importance of the Resurrection, in 1746, he published a small collection of sixteen hymns titled *Hymns for Our Lord's Resurrection*, still available in reprint.

Jesus' suffering and death have been heavily emphasized in western Christianity. His crucifixion has been a main theme of Christian painting and sculpture for many centuries. The liturgy of the Roman Catholic mass centers on his sacrificial death. In their hymns, prayers, and sermons, Protestants have likewise paid considerable attention to Jesus' death as a sacrifice for human sin. In contrast to Jesus' crucifixion, his resurrection has not been as prominent except, perhaps, during the Easter season. The Resurrection is the focus of Easter worship and is a principal theme at funeral services but is too much neglected throughout the rest of the year. Have we forgotten that we worship on Sunday, the first day of the week, to commemorate Jesus' resurrection and that our faith is rooted not only in his earthly life and death, but also in his rising from the dead?

Furthermore, we tend to forget that Jesus' crucifixion and resurrection must be understood together as a whole event. Jesus would not have been raised if he had not died. His death would have no significance for our salvation if he had not been raised from the dead (1 Corinthians 15). The four Gospel accounts underscore the relationship of both crucifixion and resurrection when they include the announcement of his resurrection after they describe his death. This hymn joyfully lifts up both Jesus' death and resurrection as central to our faith and hope.

Alleluia!

No time is inappropriate to offer God our profound thanks and adoration for the resurrection of Jesus. Easter, of course, is a special time in the church year for recalling the importance of the Resurrection. With Christians around the world and with all the host of heaven, we raise our "joys and triumphs high" as we sing "Alleluia!"

The wonder of the Easter event that inspired this hymn is captured in many places in the New Testament, but none is more notable than the description in Matthew 28. Mary Magdalene and "the other Mary" went to the tomb where Jesus' body had been laid. While they were there, the stone blocking the entrance to the tomb was incredibly rolled back. The two Marys were addressed by an angelic figure, a messenger of God, who announced that Jesus' body was no longer in the tomb. He had been raised. The angel invited the women to look at the place where his body had been placed. Then they were directed to go to the disciples and say, "He has been raised from the dead, and indeed he is going ahead of you to Galilee; there you will see him" (Matthew 28:7). Leaving the tomb in awe and with great joy, they ran to tell the disciples the good news. Their journey was interrupted by a startling meeting with the risen Jesus who repeated the instruction that his followers were to go to Galilee where he would meet them. We can imagine the disciples' amazement, surprise, and joy as the women announced to them the breathtaking news.

Wesley wrote a hymn that described Mary Magdalene's experience at the tomb and her mission to announce the good news to her friends:

> Highly favour'd Soul! to Her
>   Farther still his Grace extends,
> Raises the glad Messenger.
>   Sends her to his drooping friends:
> Tidings of their living LORD
>   First in Her Report they find:
> She must spread the Gospel-Word,
>   Teach the Teachers of Mankind.
> (Hymns for Our Lord's Resurrection, #3)

Following the directions given by the women, the disciples traveled to Galilee; met the risen Jesus; and were commissioned for a ministry of preaching, teaching, and baptizing. Furthermore, the risen Jesus promised his disciples, "I am with you always, to the end of the age" (Matthew 28:20). The same risen Christ meets us, calls us to minister in his name, and promises to accompany us in every circumstance.

"Alleluia"—the hymn's repeated response to the event of Jesus' resurrection—is the Latin form of the Hebrew word *hallelujah*, which means "praise Yah[weh]" or "praise God." Five Psalms in the Old Testament (Psalms 146–150) begin with the Hebrew word *hallelujah*, "Praise the LORD!" Each of them is a praise psalm or hymn. Appropriately, the book of Psalms closes with an expression of praise, "Let everything that breathes praise the LORD! Praise the LORD!" (Psalm 150:6). "Hallelujah" appears in only one New Testament book. The writer of Revelation envisioned a heavenly multitude joining in chorus to praise God with their "Hallelujahs" for God's "salvation and glory and power" (Revelation 19:1).

Redemption

God's redemptive work in the death and resurrection of Jesus is acclaimed in our theme hymn's second stanza. As we mentioned earlier, redemption is a concept that comes from the ancient slave market. *Redemption* was the term given to securing a slave's liberation. The one who purchased the freedom of a slave was known as the "redeemer." *Redemption* and *redeemer* are terms that appear in both Testaments (Deuteronomy 7:8; Psalm 130:8; Romans 3:24; Titus 2:14). God's love secures our redemption, our freedom, from the powerful grip of sin and death. Jesus' sacrificial death and resurrection are the means by which God's redeeming love is displayed and our redemption sealed.

In both the second and third stanzas, Wesley speaks of the struggle in which God engages forces that attempt to overcome God's purpose for our lives. It is a battle between God and his enemies, the last of which is death (1 Corinthians 15:26). Wesley portrayed Jesus as the victorious Christ in whose death God took on the powers of evil at their strongest and defeated them in raising him from the dead: "Fought the fight, the battle won." Death cannot obstruct

God's powerful plan. In his resurrection, "Christ has opened paradise" (Luke 23:43) for all who trust in him and his sacrificial death and all who call on him as their advocate (1 John 2:1-2). Another Wesley hymn proclaims the risen Christ who leads us to everlasting life:

> *The Lord of Life is ris'n indeed,*
> *To Death deliver'd in your stead;*
> *His Rise proclaims your Sins forgiven,*
> *And shews the Living Way to Heaven.*
> (Hymns for Our Lord's Resurrection, #1)

In several places in the Bible, the life of God's faithful people is described as a struggle between formidable forces of wickedness and the power of God's righteousness. The writer of the letter to Ephesians stated it succinctly: "For our struggle is not against enemies of blood and flesh, but against the rulers, against the authorities, against the cosmic powers of this present darkness, against the spiritual forces of evil in the heavenly places" (Ephesians 6:12). In this contest, we know that nothing can defeat God's purpose, not even death, because Jesus Christ has been raised (Romans 8:31-39). God's love, especially known in Jesus' death and resurrection, is the foundation of the faith in which we live and minister.

Victorious Christ

The Resurrection declares that Christ, our glorious King, lives. Death could not hold him and, therefore, cannot thwart God's plan. The second line of the third stanza, "Where, O death, is now thy sting?" is based on Paul's words in 1 Corinthians 15:54-55: "Death has been swallowed up in victory." / "Where, O death is your victory? / Where, O death, is your sting?" If someone you dearly love has died, you know the painful sting of death. Death may be a welcome relief from a devastating illness or accident for both the dying and those who care for them. No matter what the circumstances, however, death creates an agonizing emptiness in our lives. We may be angry at illness and death for taking someone who means so much to us. Perhaps we are even angry with God for allowing such destruction and death. All of us have been stung by the death of those we know and love, and we will feel its sting in our own deaths. In the face of such pain and the prospect of our own suffering and dying, because of Jesus' resurrection, we are bidden to say in faith, "Where, O death, is your sting?"

Wesley concluded the stanza with the affirmation that Jesus "died our souls to save." In light of Jesus' rising from the dead, the grave's boasting that death has defeated God is a sham. The tomb has no victory. God has defeated death in raising Jesus, our Savior and Lord.

Following Our Exalted Head

The fourth stanza of our theme hymn speaks of following Christ who has pioneered the pathway through death to everlasting life (Hebrews 12:2). Jesus has gone before us to prepare the way (John 14:1-7). God's gracious acts in the life, death, resurrection, and ascension of Jesus make it possible for us to "soar . . . where Christ has led." By his resurrection, he is our "exalted head," head of the church (Colossians 1:18) and head of each person who follows him and who bears his baptismal mark.

In another well-known hymn, Wesley offered words of praise, joy, encouragement, and exhortation to the people of the risen Christ, their "King of kings and Lord of lords" (Revelation 19:16). He reigns as their triumphant Lord; and they willingly follow him, knowing that he leads them along the way to truth and life. This path is not exempt from temptation, suffering, or death; but it is always the way to everlasting life. They proclaim, "Ours the cross, the grave, the skies."

> REJOICE, the LORD is King!
>   Your LORD and King adore,
> Mortals, give Thanks, and sing,
>   And triumph evermore;
> Lift up your Heart, lift up your Voice,
> Rejoice, again, I say, Rejoice.
>
> Jesus the Savior reigns,
>   The GOD of Truth and Love,
> When He had purg'd our Stains,
>   He took his Seat above:

Lift up your Heart, lift up your Voice,
Rejoice, again, I say, rejoice.

His Kingdom cannot fail,
He rules o'er Earth and Heaven;
The Keys of Death and Hell
Are to our JESUS given:
Lift up your Heart, lift up your Voice,
Rejoice, again, I say, Rejoice.

. . . .

Rejoice in Glorious Hope,
Jesus the Judge shall come;
And take his Servants up
To their Eternal Home:
We soon shall hear th' Archangel's Voice,
The Trump of GOD shall sound, Rejoice.
(Hymns for our Lord's Resurrection, #8)

Lord of Earth and Heaven

One of the stanzas of Wesley's "Hark! The Herald Angels Sing" begins with words of greeting, "Hail the heaven-born Prince of Peace!" Our theme hymn's fifth stanza opens with a similar salutation, "Hail the Lord of earth and heaven!" The risen Lord is worthy to be welcomed and praised by all in both realms. The New Testament writers affirm this exalted state of Christ. Their words, though words different from Wesley's words, celebrate Christ's status as the risen Son of God, the second person of the Trinity. Paul stated it this way in his Letter to the Philippians: "God . . . highly exalted him / and gave him the name that is above every name, / so that at the name of Jesus every knee should bend, / in heaven and on earth and under the earth, / and every tongue confess that Jesus Christ is Lord, / to the glory of God the Father" (Philippians 2:9-11). The risen and ascended Lord (Acts 1:6-9) is worthy of our deepest honor and adoration.

We greet the risen Christ in many ways. We meet him as we read and study Scripture, in the solitude of daily meditation and prayer, in the fellowship of worship, in the Lord's Supper, in the lives of those in need to whom we minister (Matthew 25:31-46), and in many other ways. He comes among us as the Victor over sin and death who empowers us with the Holy Spirit and the Spirit's gifts. The stanza closes with the exuberant exhortation, "Hail, the Resurrection, thou." Each and all of us are invited to rejoice in the magnificent event of God's saving action in Jesus' death and resurrection.

Another of Wesley's hymns presents the profound significance of the Resurrection and Ascension:

> *Hail the Day that sees Him rise, Alleluia!*
> *To his throne above the skies, Alleluia!*
> *Christ awhile to Mortals giv'n, Alleluia!*
> *Re-ascends his native Heav'n, Alleluia!*
>
> *There the glorious Triumph waits, Alleluia!*
> *Lift your Heads, Eternal Gates, Alleluia!*
> *Christ hath conquered Death and Sin, Alleluia!*
> *Take the King of Glory in, Alleluia!*
>
> . . . .
>
> *See! the Heavens its Lord receives, Alleluia!*
> *Yet he loves the Earth he leaves, Alleluia!*
> *Tho' returning to his Throne, Alleluia!*
> *Still he calls the World his own, Alleluia!*
>
> *See! He lifts his Hands above, Alleluia!*
> *See! He shows the Prints of Love, Alleluia!*
> *Hark! His gracious Lips bestow, Alleluia!*
> *Blessings on his Church below, Alleluia!*
> (Hymns and Sacred Poems, *pp. 211-12, altered*)

Resurrection Power and Joy

The final stanza presents a fitting close to our joyful theme hymn. Jesus' resurrection has crowned him the "King of glory." Our joy, our "soul of bliss," is rooted in his victory over sin and death. "Everlasting life" is assured through God's triumph over those forces that attempted to thwart his purpose. Wesley reminds us, however, that Jesus' resurrection is not merely an event that shapes life after death. Our present circumstances are changed by its reality and power.

"Thee to know, thy power to prove, . . . / Thus to sing, and thus to love." When Wesley spoke of *knowing* the risen Christ, it meant much more than *knowing about* him. Acquaintance with the facts of Jesus' life, teachings, deeds, death, and resurrection is important but not sufficient. When we know Jesus, we trust him to be the one through whose death and resurrection we are forgiven and guided into a life more pleasing to God. This includes Jesus' words and acts living in us, informing what we think, say, and do. By God's grace, we grow more and more into his likeness.

Christ's people live in the *power* of his resurrection. The risen Christ is the foundation for believing that nothing can separate us from God's love, not even death. No power can defeat God's purpose. This conviction is the foundation on which we live and die, witness and minister, in his name.

Surely, music is one of the great gifts of God to us. Without it, our worship and devotional life would be severely impoverished. Inspired by melodies and words, singing offers opportunities to praise God and to move through life's exhilarating and painful moments more gracefully. So, we *sing* about the victorious Christ as well as about the Father and the Holy Spirit, the trinitarian God whose image we bear.

Finally, the risen Christ moves us to acknowledge and receive in faith God's self-giving love and to offer ourselves in love to God and others, even to our enemies. This is the holiness that Charles Wesley believed is the objective of the Christian life—to love the Lord our God with all our heart, soul, mind, and strength, and our neighbors as ourselves (Leviticus 19:18; Deuteronomy 6:5; Matthew 22:37-39). It is to love God with all we are and have and to love others in the same spirit.

On Easter and every day, we sing and live our Alleluias for the risen Christ whose name we bear.

Questions for Reflection and Discussion

1. What is the importance of Jesus' resurrection?
2. What does it mean to sing, "Ours the cross, the grave, the skies" (stanza four)?

3. Charles Wesley ended this hymn speaking about love. What does love have to do with Jesus' resurrection?

4. In what ways have you felt the sting of death in your life?

5. What does it mean to say, "Christ has opened paradise" (stanza two)?

6. What is the relationship of Jesus' death to his resurrection?

Appendix

From Reluctant Priest to Extraordinary Hymn Writer

On December 18, 1707, in the Lincolnshire town of Epworth, England, Susanna Annesley Wesley gave birth to her eighteenth child, a son born prematurely. Susanna and her clergyman husband, Samuel, the Church of England rector of Epworth parish, wondered if the frail baby would survive. One biographer reported that the newborn "neither cried nor opened his eyes, and was kept wrapped up in soft wool" for some time until he could make sounds and open his eyes.[1] Samuel and Susanna named their new son Charles. They had no idea that their newest child would become one of the church's greatest hymn writers.

England, Epworth Rectory, and Childhood

The eighteenth century into which Charles Wesley was born was one of the most critical periods of England's history, a time of great change and contrast. Charles Wesley's life was significantly influenced by many of the changes.

The nation's size was growing. Its population in 1700 was approximately 5,000,000. By 1800 it increased to 8,600,000. The swelling population laid the groundwork for major economic and social development.

Through the earlier half of the eighteenth century, the English economy was principally based on farming and agriculture. By mid-century, however, it was clear that agriculture, although still important, was giving way to industrialization. The Industrial Revolution, still in its early stages, was advancing rapidly by the end of the century. A nation-wide system of canals and turnpikes facilitated the transportation of people and goods. Inventions and technological innovation spurred the growth of industry and trade. James Watt developed a new source of industrial power with his steam engine. Richard Arkwright pioneered the establishment of the modern factory system. Josiah Wedgwood, an astute industrialist, created a flourishing business through the design, manufacture, and marketing of pottery. There were countless signs of industrial transformation.

Among major economic developments was expanding trade with England's North American colonies. Regrettably, one facet of this expansion was the slave trade in which captive Africans were carried in British ships to America for sale or barter, mostly as field laborers. While Charles Wesley was a missionary to colonial Georgia in 1736, he learned firsthand the wicked nature of the slave trade and, like his brother John, came to despise it.

The growth of England's towns and cities was a consequence of industrialization. Among those that benefited most from the effects of industry were Newcastle, Manchester, Bristol, and, of course, London. As urban areas grew, problems of providing adequate housing, supplies of food and water, and hygiene intensified. Wesley not only visited many cities and towns, but also was for many years a resident of Bristol and London where he enjoyed the blessings and witnessed the despair of urban life.

The gap between rich and poor widened in eighteenth-century England. The idle rich reveled in extravagant living, entertainment, and conspicuous consumption, often at the expense of the poor. Living standards improved for the developing middle class, especially in the second half of the century. Throughout the century, however, the poor existed in wretched circumstances and found daily life both agonizing and hazardous. Charles Wesley mingled with people of all classes but was especially drawn to the poor.

Crime and corruption, sickness and death, were commonplace in eighteenth-century England. Self-serving politicians were constant pests. Crime threatened people and their property, even though a severe and sometimes cruel system of justice was set in place to stem the flow of crime, especially theft and destruction of property. The justice system often sank into inconsistent policy and political manipulation. Periodic campaigns to reform the nation's morals were launched, some of which were effective. Reform societies mobilized volunteers to address prostitution, gambling, drunkenness, and other obvious evils.

Medicine in the eighteenth century was primitive by modern standards. Epidemics of smallpox and influenza-like disease between 1727 and 1730 created the worst mortality crisis in the nation for the past 150 years. In 1753, Charles's wife, Sally, contracted smallpox. She barely survived. For several days, she was critically ill; and although smallpox did not kill her, it ruined her natural beauty, leaving her permanently scarred. As she was recovering from the illness, the couple's first son, John, contracted the disease and died.

Christianity was the official religion of England. The Church of England, or Anglican Church, was its established church, with the reigning monarch its official head. Worship in the Church of England was guided by the traditional *Book of Common Prayer*, which some Anglicans found dull and stifling. For the most part, Anglican preaching was formal and unappealing. In addition to the established Church, there were also a number of legally protected "dissenting" or "nonconformist" churches in the nation, including Quaker, Baptist, Congregationalist, and Presbyterian churches.

The Church of England, however, was the major Christian community in the nation. Two of its most devoted adherents were Samuel (1662–1735) and Susanna (1669–1742) Wesley. Both came from families of active Christians. Samuel's father, John Westley (spelled with a *t*), was an Anglican priest with nonconformist sympathies. Ordained into the Church of England priesthood, Samuel became the Rector of the Epworth parish in 1695. His parishioners found their dedicated priest a strict disciplinarian. As a result, some of them made his Epworth ministry most unpleasant. Some disgruntled members of the parish, among other misdeeds, probably set the fire that consumed the rectory (parsonage) on February 9, 1709. Like all of his siblings, one-year-old Charles survived the flames.

Samuel Wesley was a gifted scholar and poet. Among his published works were a commentary on the biblical book of Job, a lengthy poem on the life of Christ, and a hymn that survives in a number of hymnals, "Behold the Savior of Mankind." Although Samuel was a talented scholar and leader in the church, he was far from a skillful manager of household finances. In 1705, he was arrested for outstanding debts and for a short time was put in prison at Lincoln Castle, leaving the management of the family's affairs in the overworked but capable hands of Susanna.

Susanna Wesley was talented, practical, and orderly. Not only did she bear nineteen children, ten of whom (three boys and seven girls) lived into adulthood, but also she effectively managed the house, joined her husband in leading the family in devotional exercises, and daily transformed the rectory into a schoolroom in which she provided for the children's earliest education. In a letter to her son John in 1732, she outlined her exacting methods for raising and disciplining her children. By today's standards her philosophy of child-rearing would be considered excessively strict and domineering. As soon as they were able, the children were systematically taught to pray, to observe the sabbath, to read and spell, and to abide by rigorous household rules. Like his sisters and brothers, Charles received his earliest education from his mother. Susanna set aside evenings to converse with her children about God and their spiritual lives. Saturday evenings were her time with Charles.

The Wesley children were influenced profoundly by their life in the Epworth rectory. Under the guidance of Susanna and Samuel, they learned to read and appreciate the Bible, the *Book of Common Prayer*, the Lord's Prayer, and the Apostles' Creed. They were schooled in the importance of worship and the sacraments. Loyalty to the Church of England and appreciation for the significance of Christian missions and ministry were critical to their training.

In April 1716, when he was eight years old, Charles was sent to Westminster School, a private boarding school adjacent to Westminster Abbey, London. His older brother (by about sixteen years), Samuel, was a member of the staff. Under Samuel, whom he highly respected, Charles was a conscientious and devoted student. Academic excellence and the high regard in which he was held by fellow students and faculty resulted in his being chosen "Captain of the School" (head student) in 1725. Furthermore, Westminster provided the opportunity for his securing a scholarship to Christ Church, one of the prestigious colleges of Oxford University, from which both of his brothers graduated.

Holy Club, Reluctant Priest, and Missionary

Charles entered Christ Church [College] in June 1727. He enjoyed the ancient university's social atmosphere, making close friends of both men and women. According to his own account, however, he spent his first year at college "lost in diversions."[2] On one occasion, he was visited by his brother John who later wrote: "[Charles] pursued his studies diligently, and led a regular, harmless life; but if I spoke to him about religion he would warmly answer, 'What! would you have me be a saint all at once?' and would hear no more."[3] John's visit, however, proved to be a turning point for his younger brother, who thereafter vowed to be more serious about the importance of Christian faith and life.

Being an earnest Christian at Oxford University was not popular. As Charles demonstrated a religious change in his own life, he found the going difficult. He wrote:

> My standing *here* is so very slippery, no wonder I long to shift my ground. Christ Church is certainly the worst place in the world to begin a reformation in. A man stands a very fair chance of being laughed out of his religion at his first setting out, in a place where 'tis scandalous to have any at all.[4]

In search of support from other students who shared his deepening commitment to the Christian life, Charles discovered a few others who, like him, were spiritually hungry. He later described his circumstances and the origins of the group that became known as the Holy Club:

> Diligence led me into serious thinking. I went to the weekly sacrament, and persuaded two or three young scholars to accompany me, and to observe the method of study prescribed by the statutes of the University. This gained me the harmless nickname of Methodist. In half a year my Brother [John] left his curacy at Epworth, and came to our assistance. We then proceeded regularly in our studies, and in doing what good we could to the bodies and souls of men.[5]

This comment has led some to contend that Charles was the first person to be called a "Methodist," although others dispute that claim.

The Oxford Holy Club, which Charles Wesley founded and of which John Wesley became leader, involved a disciplined, demanding routine. The Holy Club linked Christian faith with holy living. In addition to early morning rising and rigorous attention to academic work, each member of the small group attended the Lord's Supper regularly, observed the church's official fasts and festivals, studied the

Bible and devotional classics, prayed together, visited the sick and imprisoned, and tutored children of the poor. From their meager student finances, the group also established a fund to assist the destitute.

One Holy Club member, George Whitefield (1714–1770), who was later ordained into the priesthood of the Church of England, became one of the most distinguished evangelical preachers in both England and America. Charles Wesley was influential in Whitefield's conversion while the latter was a Holy Club member. Although Whitefield and the Wesleys agreed on many things, including an evangelical approach to the faith, they vehemently differed on the matter of human free will. Whitefield believed that human beings have no free will to respond to God's offer of salvation. The Wesleys were certain that by God's grace all people are free to accept or reject the offer of divine forgiveness and reconciliation.

Charles's life took an unexpected turn in 1735. First, he and his family had to cope with the death of their father and all that entailed, including his mother's move out of the Epworth rectory. Second, he faced the daunting prospect of ordination into the Anglican priesthood and accompanying his brother on a mission to America. He described the unusual circumstances and his reluctance as follows:

> I took my Master's Degree, and only thought of spending all my days at Oxford. But my brother [John], who always had the ascendant over me, persuaded me to accompany him and Mr. [General James] Oglethorpe to Georgia. I exceedingly dreaded entering into holy orders: but [John] overruled me here also, and I was ordained Deacon by the Bishop of Oxford, Dr. [John] Potter, and the next Sunday, Priest, by the Bishop of London, Dr. [Edmund] Gibson.[6]

General James Oglethorpe, a member of the British Parliament, was the governor of the American colony of Georgia that he had established in 1732. It was a settlement for emigrants from Britain and the Continent. Oglethorpe desperately needed persons to help with his newly formed community. He enlisted John Wesley as a chaplain who would bring the church's ministry to the colony and chose Charles Wesley to be his personal secretary, a position for which Charles was ill equipped.

The Wesley brothers and two other members of the Holy Club, Benjamin Ingham and Charles Delamotte, sailed for America from Gravesend, England, on October 21, 1735. Poor sailing conditions forced them to lay over at the port of Cowes on the Isle of Wight off the English coast for a few weeks. Their voyage across the Atlantic did not resume until December 10. The unpleasant and hazardous journey took nearly two months. The trip was spent in the company of, among other passengers, Moravians, a community of German Christians who stressed simple faith and a personal experience of salvation. Like his brother, Charles was deeply impressed by the piety and commitment of the Moravians, not only on board the ship, but also in relationships with them that continued for a few years thereafter.

On February 5, 1736, just before setting foot on American soil, Charles wrote a despairing letter to friends back home that initially reflected the effects of the long trip and the uncertainty of the work that lay before him:

> God has brought an unhappy, unthankful wretch hither, through a thousand dangers, to renew his complaints, and loathe the life which has been preserved by a series of miracles. I take the moment of my arrival to inform you of it, because I know you will thank Him, though I cannot. I cannot, for I yet feel myself. In vain have I fled from myself to America; I still groan under the intolerable weight of inherent misery![7]

After spending a month with his brother in Savannah, Charles moved on to Frederica, a tiny coastal island settlement consisting of a fort and a few primitive huts and tents. At first, he was excited by the pastoral prospects at the tiny community. He wrote, "immediately my spirit revived. No sooner did I enter upon my ministry, than God gave me, like Saul, another heart."[8] During the ensuing months, although he experienced some satisfaction in his pastoral and administrative work, it was largely overshadowed by misery. Charles encountered serious controversy among his parishioners, described in detail in his journal. There was also tension with Oglethorpe over allegations that the governor was sexually promiscuous. Furthermore, Charles fell seriously ill with acute dysentery, a debilitating and painful disease of the digestive system.

Discouraged by the precarious state of his health and problematic relationships with some of his flock and the governor, Charles resolved to resign his position with Oglethorpe and head home to England. On July 25, 1736, he submitted his letter of resignation to the governor and within a few days bid farewell to his brother and the Georgia mission. On his way to Boston to board a ship for England, he passed through Charleston, South Carolina, where he learned about the cruel treatment of slaves. Whippings, mutilations, and murders were commonplace. His journal gives evidence of his outrage over slavery:

> It were endless to recount all the shocking instances of diabolical cruelty which these men (as they call themselves) daily practise upon their fellow creatures; and that on the most trivial occasions. . . .
>
> These horrid cruelties are the less to be wondered at, because the government itself, in effect, countenances and allows them to kill their slaves, by the ridiculous penalty appointed for it, of about seven pounds sterling, half of which is usually saved by the criminal's informing against himself. This I can look upon as no other than a public act to indemnify murder.[9]

Years later, Charles and John agreed on the demonic nature of slavery and the trade that supported it. Neither could imagine how a Christian could reconcile faith with trading or holding slaves.

Charles sailed for Boston from Charleston on August 13, 1736. The trip took more than a month, the ship docking in Boston on September 24. Two days later, a Sunday, Charles preached twice at churches in Boston. His sermon, "The One Thing Needful," based on Luke 10:42 ("One thing is needful"), was copied from a sermon written by his brother John and was later published among John's sermons.[10] The sermon provides a clue to Charles's spiritual state at the time. It speaks about the seriousness of sin and the necessity of God's image (Genesis 1:26), ruined by sin, to be renewed in every person's life, a renewal for which Charles personally yearned. The sermon closed with an exhortation:

> Let us then labor to be made perfectly whole, to burst every bond in sunder; to attain the fullest conquest over this body of death, the most entire renovation of our nature; knowing this, that when the Son of man shall send forth his angels to cast the double-minded into outer darkness, then shall the single of heart receive the one thing they sought, and shine forth as the sun in the kingdom of their Father![11]

"Singleness of heart" was not merely Wesley's wish for others. His experience in Georgia and his flight from America had raised questions about his own "singleness of heart," that is, his commitment to God and the ministry.

During his brief stay in Boston, Charles enjoyed the city and made new friends. Unfortunately, serious illness again overtook him. He graphically described it in his journal. Only with the help of a friend on October 25, 1736, did he board a ship in Boston for his return to England. After six grueling weeks crossing the Atlantic, Charles once again set foot on English soil.

Personal Pentecost, Preaching, Publishing Hymns

During the weeks that followed his homecoming, Charles was reunited with family, friends, and church officials. In an effort to satisfy and deepen his spiritual experience, he met with William Law, with whose influential writings about Christian faith and life Charles was already acquainted. Maintaining his important relationship with the Moravians, he met and conversed with Nicholas Ludwig von Zinzendorf, their principal leader, and Peter Böhler, who was about to leave on a mission to Georgia and who challenged the authenticity of Wesley's faith.

Unfortunately, ill health continued to harass Charles. Suffering through a bout of sickness on May 11, 1738, Wesley was carried to the home of a London mechanic and devoted Christian named John Bray in the hope that he would regain his physical health and, perhaps, experience a renewal of faith. The Christlike kindness and prayers of Bray and his sister, Mrs. Turner, made a decisive impression on Wesley. However, he continued to sense that his faith was lacking and that something spiritually important was missing from his life. Increasingly, Wesley suspected that he was going to encounter Christ in a new way. He was on the verge of a spiritual awakening.

Sunday, May 21, 1738, was the day of Pentecost in the church calendar. It became the day of Charles Wesley's personal Pentecost. That morning, he awoke "in hope and expectation of [Christ's] coming" to him.[12] It happened! He claimed that God "chased away the darkness of [his] unbelief." He confided to his journal, "I now found myself at peace with God, and rejoiced in hope of loving Christ. . . . I saw that by faith I stood; by the continual support of faith, which kept me from falling, though of myself I am ever sinking into sin . . .

yet confident of Christ's protection."[13] Shortly after, Wesley composed this renowned hymn celebrating his fresh meeting with God that he described as his "conversion":

Where shall my wond'ring soul begin?
How shall I all to heaven aspire?
A slave redeemed from death and sin,
A brand plucked from eternal fire,
How shall I equal triumphs raise,
Or sing my great Deliverer's praise?

O how shall I the goodness tell,
Father, which thou to me hast showed?
That I, a child of wrath and hell,
I should be called a child of God!
Should know, should feel my sins forgiven,
Blest with this antepast of heaven!

And shall I slight my Father's love?
Or basely fear his gifts to own?
Unmindful of his favors prove?
Shall I, the hallowed cross to shun,
Refuse his righteousness t'impart
By hiding it within my heart?

. . . .

Outcasts of men, to you I call,
Harlots, and publicans, and thieves!
He spreads his arms t'embrace you all
Sinners alone his grace receives:
No need of him the righteous have;
He came the lost to seek and save.

Come, O my guilty brethren, come,
Groaning beneath your load of sin;
His bleeding heart shall make you room,
His open side shall take you in.
He calls you now, invites you home—
Come, O my guilty brethren, come![14]
(A Collection of Hymns, #29)

Three days later, on May 24, 1738, John Wesley, who had returned from his own deeply disappointing mission to America earlier in the year, had a similar experience at a prayer meeting on Aldersgate Street in London and was brought by friends to Charles. They rejoiced together in John's new faith, "sang the hymn," and prayed.[15] The hymn they sang was probably the one that Charles had written just three days before. A year later, Charles wrote the hymn "For the Anniversary Day of One's Conversion." We know it as, "O For a Thousand Tongues to Sing."

Despite the overwhelming sense of God's presence and power that Charles Wesley felt the day of his personal Pentecost and that he regularly experienced for the rest of his life, he was not exempt from times of spiritual doubt and despair. Like many of us, Wesley felt the joyful assurance of God's love, forgiveness, and protection. Also like us, there were occasional times when he felt puzzled, distressed, and wondered about the depth and reality of his faith.

In the weeks and years that followed his personal Pentecost, Charles approached his ministry with new energy and enthusiasm. Spiritual and physical health improved. During the next decade, Wesley spent much of his time in an itinerant preaching ministry. He preached in churches, homes, and in the open air. His journal and letters provide much detail about this period of his life.

Although Charles is widely acclaimed for his poetic talents, he was also an outstanding preacher. His preaching, like his hymns, was thoroughly saturated with the Bible. Furthermore, his skill with language, both prose and poetry, strengthened his proclamation of the gospel. Some said he was a better preacher than John. One of Charles's listeners asserted that "he had a remarkable talent of expressing the most important truths with simplicity and energy; and his discourses [sermons] were sometimes truly apostolic, forcing conviction on the hearers in spite of the most determined opposition."[16]

Charles Wesley claimed that in some locations thousands of persons came to hear him preach. Many who listened were changed by God under his speaking God's word. His skillful and effective preaching was a major factor in the early growth of Methodism. Unfortunately, few of his sermons survive; but it is certain from those that remain, as well as from testimonies of his listeners, that his preaching centered on the main tenets of Christianity.

On Sunday, July 1, 1739, Charles preached a sermon on Romans 3:23-25 to a university congregation in Oxford. The manuscript of the sermon has been preserved and illustrates some of the principal themes of the evangelical faith that he regularly declared. The sermon speaks of the seriously sinful and fallen state in which all humans exist apart from God, a state in which they are spiritually destitute and stand under God's exacting judgment. Yet, God's love seeks to reconcile them in Christ's atoning death. Jesus' sacrifice on the cross makes possible forgiveness and new life. Trusting in God's grace, displayed in Jesus, justifies us before God and brings us peace with God. This faith works by love, love for God and for neighbor, manifested in holiness of heart and life.

One of the special areas of Charles's ministry was preaching to and providing pastoral care for prisoners, among the most despised people of the time. This ministry began as early as his student days in the Holy Club. In July 1738, Wesley made several visits to the infamous Newgate prison in London to meet the prisoners and to preach to them. Descriptions of these occasions are moving. His journal records some of them in detail.

> Wed., July 12th. I preached at Newgate to the condemned felons, and visited one of them in his cell, sick of a fever; a poor black that had robbed his master. I told him of one who came down from heaven to save lost sinners, and him in particular; described the sufferings of the Son of God, his sorrows, agony, and death. He listened with all the signs of eager astonishment; the tears trickled down his cheeks while he cried, "What! was it for me? Did God suffer all this for so poor a creature as me?" I left him waiting for the salvation of God.[17]

Charles's caring ministry to this prisoner and others awaiting execution resulted in their acceptance of Christ. Some prisoners were brought from their Newgate cells to Tyburn, London's place of public hanging, on July 19, 1738. Charles was there. At Tyburn, he mounted the hangman's cart with two friends and prayed with the prisoners he had met at Newgate. Wesley reported that the convicts were "full of comfort, peace, and triumph; assuredly persuaded Christ had died for them, and wanted to receive them into paradise." At the appropriate time, Wesley and his friends dismounted from the cart, and it was driven away from the gallows, causing the prisoners to die as they hung from their nooses. Charles reported that he felt great compassion for them and was confident that their newly confessed faith won them a place of comfort and peace in God's kingdom.[18] This was one of countless incidents during which Wesley witnessed the power of God's presence and grace at work in the lives of desperately needy people. Convinced that God's grace was available to all, he proclaimed salvation in Christ, assurance, new birth, and sanctification to all who came to hear him.

Not all who heard Charles were moved to accept the gospel message he announced. Some were troubled by his plain speaking about sin, the necessity of repentance, the experience of assurance, and the expectation of holy living. They thought that baptism and regular (or even occasional) church attendance were sufficient. Not according to Charles and the Methodists! Others were put off by some of Charles's "irregularities." He preached in places other than church buildings—even in the open air—a radical practice for the time. His encouragement of congregational hymn singing was suspect. Still others were convinced that Charles and John were undermining the ministry of the Church of England by organizing their Methodist followers into societies and smaller units called classes. The Wesleys' intent, of course, was not to weaken the Church of England, but to fortify it. Methodists were admonished to be faithful to their church, its doctrine, liturgy, and sacraments; but they were also expected to attend weekly Methodist society and class meetings. Methodism was a demanding and disciplined pathway of Christian worship and discipleship. Nevertheless, some interpreted Methodism as a threat to both church and social order.

In the early 1740s especially, Charles Wesley and the Methodists were confronted with verbal and violent opposition, some of it inspired by clergy and church leaders. Charles's journal recorded several dangerous situations in which he was assaulted by threatening mobs. On Friday, July 22, 1743, he was preaching in a home at St. Ives, a small town in Cornwall, on the text, "Comfort ye, comfort ye my people, saith your God" (Isaiah 40:1):

> when an army of rebels broke in upon us, like those at Sheffield or Wednesbury. They began in a most outrageous manner, threatening to murder the people, if they did not go out that moment. They broke the sconces, dashed the windows in pieces, tore away the shutters, benches, poor-box, and all but the stone-walls. I stood silently looking on; but mine eyes were unto the Lord. They swore bitterly I should not preach there again; which I disproved, by immediately telling them Christ died for them all. Several times they lifted up their hands and clubs to strike me; but [God's] stronger arm restrained them. They beat and dragged the women about, particularly one of a great age, and trampled on them without mercy. The longer they stayed, and the more they raged, the more power I found from above. I bade

the people stand still and see the salvation of God; resolving to continue with them, and see the end. In about an hour the word came, "Hitherto shalt thou come, and no farther." The ruffians fell to quarreling among themselves, broke the Town-Clerk's (their captain's) head, and drove one another out of the room.[19]

In other places Wesley was attacked with sticks and pelted with eggs, stones, and dirt. A concerted effort by some, including a few Anglican clergy, aimed to keep Methodists from meeting and Charles from preaching. Being a "Methodist" in the 1740s in some places was neither prudent nor safe. Charles was not deterred, however, either by the threats or by the attacks on him as he carried out God's work. Over the succeeding decades, even though he and the Methodist movement were mistrusted by some, the severest persecution ended.

Although Charles was apparently an impressive preacher, his most important contribution to Methodism and the Evangelical Revival of the eighteenth century was his hymns. For these he wrote the poetry, not the music. There are various estimates as to how many hymns he wrote, some as high as nine thousand.

Evidence of Charles's early musical training and interests is scant. He undoubtedly participated in singing in the Epworth rectory, in his father's church, at Westminster School, and at Christ Church. During and after the Georgia mission, the music of the Moravians was a strong influence on his life. His musical and poetic talents were formed by these and other forces. Charles's journal mentions countless occasions of his singing with congregations, with smaller groups in homes, and even with prisoners in their cells.

Charles's hymn-poems were written over several decades. Many were published in hymnbooks that were edited by his brother John. Beginning in the 1740s, Charles published a few small collections of his hymns for the church year, including *Hymns for the Nativity of Our Lord* (1745), *Hymns on the Lord's Supper* (1745), *Hymns for Ascension-Day* (1746), and *Hymns for our Lord's Resurrection* (1746). From 1750 to 1780, his hymn writing continued to be productive. One of the most important published collections of this period was *Hymns on the Trinity* (1767). Charles was convinced that his hymns should emphasize the love of God, especially known in Jesus Christ. He wrote:

JESUS *the Soul of Musick is;*
His is the Noblest Passion:
JESUS' *Name is Joy and Peace,*
Happiness and Salvation:
JESUS' *Name the Dead can raise,*
Shew us our Sins forgiven,
Fill us with all the Life of Grace,
Carry us up to Heaven.[20]

One very important, substantial, and widely used Methodist hymn-book, titled *A Collection of Hymns for the Use of the People Called Methodists*, published in 1780, included hymns by several writers; but over 475 of them were written by Charles.

During the 1740s, Wesley became involved in two major theological controversies. The first was a dispute with the Moravians. Although he was friendly with, and influenced by, Moravians since his days in Georgia, he was increasingly critical of their urging persons who were not Christians to wait *passively* for the redeeming working of God, thereby neglecting "the means of grace" that, Charles asserted, Christ urges us to employ. Displaying his intense disagreement with the passive, or "stillness," view, Charles wrote:

> The unjustified, say [the Moravians], are *to be still*; that is, not to search the Scriptures, not to pray, not to [receive the Lord's Supper], not to do good, not to endeavor, not to desire; for it is impossible to use [the] means [of grace] without trusting in them. Their practice is agreeable to their principles. Lazy and proud themselves, bitter and censorious toward others, they trample upon the ordinances, and despise the commands, of Christ. I see no middle point where we can meet.[21]

Wesley was persuaded that God provided "means of grace," such as prayer, fasting, Bible study, and the Lord's Supper, to convey saving and empowering grace in to people's lives. These essential means of grace should be used as Christ directed.

The second controversy was equally, if not more, serious to the progress of the Wesleyan movement: Was divine saving grace available to all human beings ("universal redemption") or only to a select number? Did all humans have freedom to accept or reject God's offer of forgiveness and new life? Furthermore, when someone accepted God's salvation, was it possible to lose it, that is, to fall from grace?

These were questions with which Charles Wesley dealt throughout the decade of the 1740s and later. He believed these questions were clearly answered by Scripture and the church's doctrines.

By God's grace, Wesley argued, salvation is offered to all. By God's grace, everyone is free to embrace or refuse redemption and renewal offered in the life, death, and resurrection of Jesus. Wesley maintained, however, that everyone was required to exercise trusting faith in God in order to receive salvation. He also held that believers are always free by their thoughts, words, and acts to turn away from God and to lose their salvation. Charles's hymn texts provide adequate evidence of his views on these questions. The following two stanzas of a hymn of invitation, for example, address his dedication to announce God's universal love for all:

> *Come, sinners, to the gospel feast;*
> *Let every soul be Jesu's guest;*
> *Ye need not one be left behind,*
> *For God hath bidden all mankind.*

> *Sent by my Lord, on you I call;*
> *The invitation is to all:*
> *Come all the world; come, sinner, thou!*
> *All things in Christ are ready now.*[22]

Throughout the 1740s, Charles was an energetic traveling preacher. It is difficult for us who are accustomed to modern, accessible, and well-paved roads and various means of transportation to appreciate the difficulty with which people traveled in the eighteenth century. Although there were noticeable road improvements, mostly to the main thoroughfares, roads remained dusty in dry weather and quagmires when wet. Deep ruts carved by wagons and coaches made riding horseback precarious. There was always concern about the health and capability of one's horse. During the decade of the 1740s, Charles traveled thousands of miles on these roads in all sorts of weather. In addition to his travel in England and Wales, he also sailed to Ireland in 1747 to begin Methodist preaching, the first of several trips to the Irish. The consuming task of this travel was preaching the gospel and organizing and nurturing Methodist societies, visiting the sick and imprisoned, and acting as Christ's emissary in every possible way.

The decade of the 1740s was significant for other reasons. On July 30, 1742, his mother, Susanna, died. John Wesley reported that a group stood around her bed at the time of her death and fulfilled her final request that they "sing a psalm of praise to God."[23] Two days later, her body was buried, a stone placed at the head of her grave inscribed with commemorative words written by Charles. One of the most influential persons in his life was gone.

Two years later, Charles was present at the Foundery, the converted canon factory and principal Methodist meeting house in London, where he joined his brother and eight others in the first annual conference of the Methodist preachers. The group discussed matters of doctrine, discipline, and practice. They pledged their loyalty to the Church of England, reasserting that Methodism's mission was to strengthen the Church of England, not to weaken it. This had always been Charles's intention and remained a principal aim of his ministry. He was willing to spend his life for Methodism as it supported the church that he loved and into which he was ordained.

Marriage, Family, Controversy

A major turning point in Charles Wesley's life began in August, 1747, when he met Sarah Gwynne. Sarah's family, who resided in Garth, a small town in Wales, was prosperous and prominent. More important, they were committed to Methodism. Although Charles was nineteen years older than Sarah, they were almost instantly drawn to each other; and courtship began. As the relationship matured, Charles spoke of Sarah (he called her Sally) as his "dearest friend" and was finally convinced that they should marry. Sally was willing; but her family, especially her mother, needed to be convinced that Charles could adequately provide for her. After all, although he was an upstanding Anglican priest, he had no settled parish and a somewhat uncertain income. Vincent Perronet, one of Charles's closest friends, persuaded the Gwynnes that even though Charles was not wealthy, his share of the Wesley brothers' income from their many publications was more than sufficient to care for Sally and any family born to them. With this satisfaction, the Gwynnes gave their blessing to the marriage, and the couple were united on April 8, 1749, in a ceremony conducted by his brother John. In his journal,

Charles claimed that the bride and groom began their wedding day with more than three hours of prayer and singing.

Charles's marriage, unlike that of his brother John's, was characterized by deep love for his wife. Their marital partnership prospered in the midst of his rigorous schedule of preaching and pastoral travel. It was not easy for either of them to cope with lengthy periods of absence while Charles fulfilled his commitments to the growing Methodist movement. Letters to Sally and journal entries make clear that his love for her, and hers for him, sustained them during those trying times.

A greater degree of stability for Charles and Sally commenced on September 1, 1749, when they moved into their own home in Bristol. Although the couple's life together was more settled, it was not without difficulty. Shortly after moving to Bristol, Charles was embroiled in a situation regarding John's impending marriage to Grace Murray, one of their faithful Methodist followers. For various reasons, Charles was convinced that the proposed marriage was not a match made in heaven. His interference led to Grace's marriage to another Methodist preacher, John Bennett, which aroused John Wesley's bitterest anger. John's fury with his brother in the matter caused Charles to respond in kind, "I renounce all intercourse with you but what I would have with a heathen and a publican."[24] It appeared that relations between the brothers would never be the same.

Less than two years later, in 1751, yet another incident upset Charles. In February 1751, John suddenly entered into a matrimonial venture with a wealthy widow, Mary Vazeille. Charles was extremely wary of the marriage. Although he and Sally seem to have made serious attempts to be amiable with their new sister-in-law, the relationship was difficult. As it turned out, the marriage was one of John's (and his wife's) major mistakes.

There were other, more painful, events in Charles's Bristol home. In December 1753, Sally contracted smallpox and lay near death for several days. Although she recovered, the disease left her with unsightly scars that disfigured her body. She had barely recovered when their son, Jacky (John Wesley Jr.), became a smallpox victim and died. Charles and Sally were distraught. The couple lost five more children in infancy and early childhood. When Charles later wrote hymns about the sickness and death of children, he knew personally the agony of losing a child.

Three children born to the marriage survived into adulthood: Charles Wesley Jr., Samuel, and Sarah, sometimes called Sally Jr. Both of the sons exhibited remarkable musical talents from their earliest years. Their parents did what they could to nurture their gifts, even sponsoring the boys in concert in the Wesley home. Charles Jr., an organist, was later employed in London churches. His more accomplished brother, Samuel, loved formal liturgy and cathedral music and, to the displeasure of his father, converted to Roman Catholicism. Sally Jr. was intellectually bright and brought her parents great joy. In one letter, her father referred to himself as "My dear Sally's father and friend."[25] Although her connections with Methodism were not strong, in religion, she was more like her parents than her brothers were.

Bouts of ill health and commitment to a more settled family life forced Charles to lessen his travel. In 1771, he moved the family to London, where they occupied a comfortable home at 1 Great Chesterfield Street in Marylebone, then a pleasant suburb of the city.

In the meantime, however, with his brother, Charles continued to deal with controversies in the Methodist ranks. Two of them involved the relationship of Methodism to the Church of England. The first concerned the status and role of lay preachers in the Methodist movement. As Methodism took root in the 1730s and 1740s, lay preachers with suitable talents for preaching and pastoral care became indispensable leaders in the movement. Recognizing the critical role these preachers occupied, Charles was increasingly persuaded that they must be qualified and effective in their ministry. He was convinced that "no one be allowed to preach with us, till my brother and I have heard him with our own ears, and talked fully with him, and if needs [be] to keep him with us some days."[26] Those who were unsatisfactory must not be admitted to the Methodist ministry. Those who proved ineffective or immoral and who refused to abide by Methodist discipline and doctrine were to be dismissed, as were those who undermined Methodism's connection to the Church of England. With John's blessing, Charles set about to purge the movement of those lay preachers who did not meet Methodist standards, who pressed to administer the sacraments, and who threatened Methodism's Anglican affiliation. He discharged those whom he found unacceptable.

A second controversy centered more directly on the Wesleys' and Methodism's kinship with the national church. Charles was determined that the Methodist movement must not separate from the Church of England. From the earliest days, he voiced his fear that Methodism might become a "sect," a religious body separate from England's established church rather than an integral part of it. He never surrendered this apprehension. It is not surprising, therefore, that Charles was increasingly disturbed by the actions of John that Charles was convinced would lead to Methodism's separation from Anglicanism. His worst fears were realized in September 1784, when John ordained two of his lay preachers, Richard Whatcoat and Thomas Vasey. John also ordained an Anglican priest, Thomas Coke, to be "superintendent" of Methodist work in America, which conferred on Coke the authority to ordain others into the ministry. John then dispatched Whatcoat, Vasey, and Coke to America with orders to form a new church. To Charles, these ordinations were proof of the Methodist separation from the Anglican Church. He was deeply troubled by John's acting as an Anglican bishop, and his famous (or infamous) couplet sarcastically voiced his displeasure:

> *So easily are Bishops made*
> *By man's, or woman's whim?*
> *W[esley] his hands on C[oke] hath laid,*
> *But who laid hands on Him?*[27]

John denied that what he said and did would cause Methodism to separate from the Church of England, except for America. Charles felt otherwise. His deep pain is clear in his famous letter to Dr. Chandler. Speaking of John, Charles wrote: "Thus our Partnership here is dissolved, but not our Friendship. I have taken him for better or worse, till death do us part; or rather, re-unite us in love inseparable. I have lived on earth a little too long—who have lived to see this evil day."[28] Nevertheless, Charles continued to preach in Methodist meetings and urged Methodists not to separate from the Church of England. Except in America, separation from the Anglican Church did not come in the Wesleys' lifetime.

Another major brotherly disagreement arose over the doctrine of entire sanctification or Christian perfection. From its earliest days, Methodism, nurtured by the leadership of the Wesley brothers, emphasized sanctification (holiness of heart and life) leading to entire sanctification or Christian perfection. Yet, as early as 1767, it became apparent that the brothers had different views on Christian perfection. On the one hand, John thought of perfection as perfect love for God and neighbor that led the believer to conform to God's will. Although perfect love might be attained gradually—that is, growing in grace—it could also be an instantaneous gift of God, an infusion of God's love, which resulted in purity of heart. By God's grace, Christian perfection of this sort was possible, even instantaneously, in this earthly life. On the other hand, Charles was convinced that Christian perfection included the removal of sin and the restoration of God's image (Genesis 1:26) in the believer. It was gradual, never instantaneous, and would only be fully realized at the time of death, on the threshold between earthly life and life in the world to come. Charles held that this understanding of Christian perfection was taught by the early Christian church. Furthermore, he was fearful that one's claim of perfect love for God and neighbor in this life would inevitably lead to spiritual pride. He worried about those who thought that continued growth was unnecessary and considered themselves better than others. He voiced his reservations about those who professed Christian perfection in a letter to Joseph Cownley, "You believe a man perfect because he says 'I am': that's the very reason for which I believe, and am sure, he is not perfect."[29]

Closing Years

By the late-1770s, Charles was still writing poetry; visiting London's Newgate prison; preaching twice on Sundays at Methodism's City Road Chapel, London, which opened in 1778; and engaging in other pastoral work. In spite of advancing age and growing health problems, he was determined to continue his ministry. In a 1779 letter to John, he boasted about his preaching. "Last Sunday I preached twice, never with greater power, and seldom with equal effect."[30] He also managed to make occasional visits to Methodist work outside London, riding to Bristol as few as five months prior to his death.

Although Charles and John had their differences over the years, some of which were quite serious, they remained partners in ministry to the end. When he learned in February 1788, that his brother was desperately ill, John wrote to him with suggestions to improve his health. The worn-out preacher, however, was not to recover this time. He dictated his final poem to his wife, Sally:

In age and feebleness extreme,
Who shall a helpless worm redeeem?
Jesus! my only hope Thou art,
Strength of my failing flesh and heart;
Oh! could I catch one smile from Thee
And drop into eternity![31]

Charles's daughter, Sally, sent a letter to her uncle John, in which she described her father's last days. According to Sally, when one visitor said to Charles "that the valley of the shadow of death was hard" to pass, her father replied, "Not with Christ."[32] In that spirit Charles Wesley died on March 29, 1788, at his home in London. With great sadness, Charles's family and friends attended his funeral at Marylebone church.

John Wesley was deeply distressed by his brother's death. His closest partner in the Methodist movement was now absent. About two weeks later he was preaching at Bolton, a town in Lancashire. Attempting to teach the congregation his brother's hymn "Come, O Thou Traveler Unknown," he burst into tears when he came to the line, "My company before is gone, and I am left alone with thee."

Of the many recollections of Charles by his family and friends, none is more revealing than the words of his physician, Dr. John Whitehead, who said of Charles:

Mr. Wesley was of a warm and lively disposition; of great frankness and integrity, and generous and steady in his friendships. . . . In conversation he was pleasing, instructive, and cheerful; and his observations were often seasoned with wit and humor. His religion was genuine and unaffected. As a minister, he was familiarly acquainted with every part of divinity [theology]; and his mind was furnished with an uncommon knowledge of the Scriptures. His discourses from the pulpit were not dry and systematic, but flowed from the present views and feelings of his own mind. . . .

The Methodists are greatly indebted to him for his unwearied labors and great usefulness at the first formation of the societies, when every step was attended with difficulty and danger. And being dead he yet speaketh, by his numerous and excellent hymns, written for the use of the societies, which still continue to be the means of daily edification to thousands.[33]

Sarah Wesley, Charles's wife, outlived him by almost thirty-four years, dying on December 22, 1822. By that time, Methodists and

Christians in many other denominations were regularly lifting their voices to God with her husband's hymns.

Questions for Reflection and Discussion

1. What did you know about Charles Wesley before reading this biography? What have you learned by reading this account of Wesley's life?

2. What surprised you about Charles Wesley's life and ministry?

3. Charles Wesley was influenced by his environment (nation, church, home, schooling, friends, marriage and family, and so forth). In what ways does your environment shape you and influence your faith?

4. Prisons and prisoners were a major concern of Charles Wesley throughout his ministry. How might you be involved in such a ministry today?

5. Have you experienced a "personal Pentecost" like Wesley's?

6. Charles Wesley and his brother John had serious disagreements on several occasions that threatened their relationship. What held them together?

Notes

1. Thomas Jackson, *The Life of the Rev. Charles Wesley, M.A.* (New York: Lane and Sandford, 1844), 21.

2. Letter to Dr. Chandler, April 28, 1785.

3. Quoted in Frank Baker, *Charles Wesley As Revealed in His Letters* (London: Epworth Press, 1948), 10.

4. Letter, January 22, 1729. The letter was begun on January 5, 1729.

5. Letter to Dr. Chandler, April 28, 1785.

6. Ibid.

7. Letter to Sally Kirkham, February 5, 1736.

8. Journal entry, March 9, 1736.

9. Journal entry, August 2, 1736.

10. See Sermon #146 in Albert C. Outler, editor, *Sermons IV, The Works of John Wesley*, Vol. 4, 351-59.

11. Ibid., 359.

12. Journal entry, May 21, 1738.

13. Ibid.

14. Franz Hildebrandt and Oliver A. Beckerlegge, eds., *A Collection of Hymns for the Use of The People Called Methodists*, Vol. 7, *The Works of John Wesley* (Nashville: Abingdon Press, 1983), 116-117.

15. Journal entry, May 21, 1738.

16. John Whitehead, *Life of the Rev. John Wesley . . . with The Life of the Rev. Charles Wesley* (London: Stephen Couchman, 1893), Vol. I, 370.

17. Journal entry, July 12, 1738.

18. Journal entry, July 19, 1738.

19. Journal entry, July 22, 1743.

20. Frank Baker, *Representative Verse of Charles Wesley* (Nashville: Abingdon Press, 1962), 118.

21. Journal entry, April 25, 1740.

22. Hildebrandt and Beckerlegge, 81. Emphasis added.

23. W. Reginald Ward and Richard P. Heitzenrater, eds., *Journal and Diaries II*, Vol. 19, *The Works of John Wesley* (Nashville: Abingdon Press, 1990), 283.

24. Quoted in Frederick C. Gill, *Charles Wesley: The First Methodist* (Nashville: Abingdon, 1964), 148.

25. Letter to Sally, Jr., October 11, 1777.

26. Letter to Lady Huntingdon, August 4, 1752. It is believed that this letter was probably written earlier.

27. Quoted in John R. Tyson, ed., *Charles Wesley: A Reader* (New York: Oxford University Press, 1989), 429.

28. Letter to Dr. Chandler, April 28, 1785.

29. Quoted in Baker, 120.

30. Quoted in Gill, 220.

31. Tyson, 481.

32. Ibid.

33. Ibid., 482-83.

Bibliography

Baker, Frank. *Charles Wesley, as Revealed by His Letters*. London: Epworth Press, 1948.

———. *Charles Wesley's Verse: An Introduction*. London: Epworth Press, 1964.

Dallimore, Arnold A. *A Heart Set Free: The Life of Charles Wesley*. Westchester, Ill.: Crossway Books, 1988.

Gill, Frederick C. *Charles Wesley: The First Methodist*. New York: Abingdon Press, 1964.

Hildebrandt, Franz, and Oliver A. Beckerlegge, eds.. *A Collection of Hymns for the Use of the People Called Methodists*. The Works of John Wesley, vol. 7. Nashville: Abingdon Press, 1983.

Jackson, Thomas, ed. *The Journal of Charles Wesley, M.A.* Reprint. Grand Rapids: Baker Book House, 1980. Sections of the Journal are also available on the following Web site: http://wesley.nnu.edu.

Kimbrough, S T, Jr., ed. *Charles Wesley: Poet and Theologian*. Nashville: Kingswood Books, 1992.

———. *A Heart to Praise My God: Wesley Hymns for Today*. Nashville: Abingdon Press, 1996.

———. *Songs for the Poor: Hymns by Charles Wesley*. New York: General Board of Global Ministries, 1997.

Kimbrough, S T, Jr., and Oliver A Beckerlegge, eds. *The Unpublished Poetry of Charles Wesley*. Three vols. Nashville: Kingswood Books, 1988–1992.

Lawson, John. *The Wesley Hymns as a Guide to Scriptural Teaching*. Grand Rapids: F. Asbury Press, 1987.

Newport, Kenneth G. C. *The Sermons of Charles Wesley: A Critical Edition with Introduction and Notes*. New York: Oxford University Press, 2001.

Osborn, G., ed. *The Poetical Works of John and Charles Wesley*. 13 vols. (London: Wesleyan-Methodist Conference Office, 1868–1872).

Rattenbury, J. Ernest. *The Eucharistic Hymns of John and Charles Wesley*. London: Epworth Press, 1948.

———. *The Evangelical Doctrines of Charles Wesley's Hymns*. London: Epworth, 1942.

Routley, Erik. *The Musical Wesleys*. New York: Oxford University Press, 1968.

Tyson, John R., ed. *Charles Wesley: A Reader*. New York: Oxford University Press, 1989.

Tyson, John R. *Charles Wesley on Sanctification: A Biographical and Theological Study*. Grand Rapids: F. Asbury Press, 1986.

Wesley, Charles. *Hymns for Ascension-Day and Hymns for Whitsunday*. Reprint Madison, N.J.: Charles Wesley Society, 1994.

———. *Hymns on the Great Festivals and Other Occasions*. Reprint. Madison, N.J.: Charles Wesley Society, 1996.

———. *Hymns on the Lord's Supper*. Reprint. Madison, N.J.: Charles Wesley Society, 1995.

———. *Hymns for the Nativity of Our Lord*. Reprint. Madison, N.J.: Charles Wesley Society, 1991.

———. *Hymns for Our Lord's Resurrection*. Reprint. Madison, N.J.: Charles Wesley Society, 1992.

———. *Hymns on the Trinity*. Reprint. Madison, N.J.: Charles Wesley Society, 1998.

Wesley, John and Charles Wesley. *Hymns and Sacred Poems*. London: William Strahan, 1739.

Wesley Center Online, http://wesley.nnu.edu.

Young, Carlton R. *Music of the Heart: John and Charles Wesley on Music and Musicians*. Carol Stream, Ill.: Hope Publishing Company, 1995.

(The reprints published by the Charles Wesley Society may be ordered from them at P.O. Box 127, Madison, NJ 07940-0127.)